Praise for *The Lan*

"Blomfield has written a remarkab
sion of Shi'ism is dominated by Ira. ... ~~~~~cs, sectarianism,
and male Ayatollahs. Blomfield takes us inside another world,
the world of a mystical, every day encounters of Shi'i women.
Recommended to Islamic studies, women's studies, and Middle
Eastern studies audiences."

–Omid Safi, author of *Memories of Muhammad*

"Honest, engaging, and insightful, *The Language of Tears* is touch-
ing, inspiring, and entertaining. Bridget Blomfield's captivating
account of her journey inside the inner-world of Shi'ite women,
from Iraqi, Iranian, and Indo-Pakistani origin, moved me to
both tears and laughter. A must-read for anyone who wishes to
understand how Shi'ism is experienced by women in East and
West and those who have formed a bridge between both worlds."

–John Andrew Morrow, author of *The Covenants of the
Prophet Muhammad with the Christians of the World*

"A delightful read and gently illuminating memoir of some five
years spent with Shi'i women associated with a Muslim parochial
school in southern California, *The Language of Tears* is a counter
to the bad press we too often see about Muslims and Islam. . . . We
get to know these Muslim women and girls as believers, devoted
to family, and caring community members. We see how emotional intimacy with the Shi'i saints and community ties with other
women foster a sense of belonging and acceptance. The description
of differences between the younger American-raised females and
their elders is fascinating. The young can be 'hip and cool, pious
and punk,' self-proclaimed feminists, and planning for both family
and career in their futures. The book is an excellent introduction
to Shi'i Islam that is not pedantic or academic. The book also will
appeal to the intelligent reader who wants to better understand this
religion—so significant in the world today—as regular, religious
insiders see and feel it."

–Mary Elaine Hegland, author of *Days of Revolution:
Political Struggle in an Iranian Village*

"In examining women's rituals in American Shi'ite Muslim communities, Bridget Blomfield has been able to connect what appear to be strictly religious rituals to contemporary politics; with immigrant issues including racism, sexism, and attitudes towards Muslims and Arabs in the post-9/11 context; with generational gap issues between immigrant parents and their children raised in North America; and with gender issues in a highly shari'ah-conscious community. At the same time, she has been able to access the textual and religious and normative understandings these particular communities have of their own theological and ritual discourses. *The Language of Tears* provides a rare glimpse into the lives, concerns, and world views of migrant communities caught in larger geopolitical currents."

–Zayn Kassam, Professor of Religious Studies, Pomona College

"Today, sadly, there is so much distrust and prejudice in Western societies about Muslims. In her very personal and heartfelt book, Bridget Blomfield takes us on a journey into the lives of Shi'a women pursuing their faith in Southern California. The author's unique gift is the depth to which she could set herself aside and allow herself to be guided, challenged, teased, and ultimately embraced by the women she came to study. This is a book about the pride, commitment, and humanity of these women and how the author gained their trust and was initiated into many of their most profound rituals."

–Richard Moss, M.D. author of *The Black Butterfly* and *The Mandala of Being*

"Bridget Blomfield's *The Language of Tears* provides an insider's perspective of the symbols enacted and the rituals undertaken by Shi'i women, both in their mosques and homes in America. Few Western scholars have had access to these quarters. She is the first scholar to have entered and described the sacred space and mourning rituals of Shi'i women in America. Her portrayal, discussion, and analysis of rituals and their symbolic effects is incisive and informative."

–Professor Liyakat Takim, McMaster University, Sharjah Chair in Global Islam

The Language *of* Tears

The
Language
of Tears

My Journey into the World
of Shi'i Muslim Women

BRIDGET BLOMFIELD

WHITE CLOUD PRESS
ASHLAND, OREGON

White Cloud Press titles may be purchased for educational, business, or sales promotional use. For information, please write:

Special Market Department
White Cloud Press
PO Box 3400, Ashland, OR 97520
Website: www.whitecloudpress.com

Cover and interior design by C Book Services
Printed in the United States of America

15 16 17 18 19 20   10 9 8 7 6 5 4 3 2 1

Library of Congress Cataloging-in-Publication Data
Blomfield, Bridget.
    The language of tears : my journey into the world of Shi'i muslim women / Bridget Blomfield.
        pages cm. -- (Islamic encounter series)
    Includes bibliographical references and index.
    ISBN 978-1-935952-42-8 (paperback)
    1. Women in Islam. 2. Muslim women. 3. Shi'ah--California. 4. Blomfield, Bridget. 5. Teachers--California--Biography. I. Title.
    BP173.4.B56 2015
    297.8'2082--dc23
                                        2015009065

Dedication

This book is dedicated to all men, women and children who have suffered at the hands of an oppressor yet managed to live with faith, hope and love. May justice prevail.

Acquire knowledge, because he who acquires it in the way of the Lord performs an act of piety; who speaks of it, praises the Lord; who seeks it, adores God; who dispenses instruction in it, bestows alms; and who imparts it to its fitting objects, performs an act of devotion to God. Knowledge enables its possessor to distinguish what is forbidden from what is not; it lights the way to Heaven; it is our friend in the desert, our society in solitude, our companion when bereft of friends; it guides us to happiness; it sustains us in misery; it is our ornament in the company of friends; it serves as an armor against our enemies. With knowledge, the obedient servant of God rises to the heights of goodness and to a noble position, associates with sovereigns in this world, and attains to the perfection of happiness in the next.

–The Prophet Muhammad

Surely hearts have desires, and they turn towards, and they turn away . . . so approach them by means of what they desire and what they turn towards, for surely if the heart is forced to do some thing against its will, it goes blind.

–Imam Ali

Contents

Introduction: The Language of Tears   xi

1. The City of Knowledge: Learning
about Islam through the Eyes of Children   1

2. Fatima: Lady of Heaven   17

3. Zaynab: Young Women and Feminism   33

4. Muharram   56

5. The Iranian Women   75

6. The Iraqi Women   90

7. The Pakistani/Indian Women   107

Epilogue   131

Glossary   157

Acknowledgment

I would first and foremost like to thank Dr. Zayn Kassam and Dr. Barbara Aswad for their continued support through my dissertation process and finally this book. Thanks to Dr. Hamid Mavani for steering me into the academic world of Shi'ism. Thanks also to Dr. Wilma Heckler my friend and mentor. I owe much gratitude to Steve Scholl for his eternal patience and encouragement. Special thanks to Dr. Haleema Shaikley and the women from the City of Knowledge School who poured endless cups of tea while they shared with me their stories so beautiful and poignant. They showed me the lived experience of Shi'ism and treated me like a sister. May our hearts be joined throughout eternity.

Introduction

While pursuing a PhD in religious studies at Claremont Graduate University in 2002, I decided to study Arabic. At that time, there were no Arabic classes offered at the university I attended. Remembering that I had seen a *masjid* (the correct name for a mosque) and an Islamic school near my home, I got into the car and started my search for such lessons. Eventually I came to an intersection and I had to make a choice; for some unknown reason I chose to turn left. I later discovered that if I had turned right, I would have come upon a Sunni masjid. By turning left I ended up at an Islamic school run by Shi'a Muslims. The Shi'a represent approximately 15 to 20 percent of the world's Muslim population; the other 80 percent are Sunni. Shi'a are to Islam what Catholics are to Christianity, sharing similar rituals. I didn't really know the difference between these two approaches to Islam until I went to the school. Little did I know that I had come to a critical intersection and that my doctoral dissertation would be written about the women I met at the school.

As I pulled into the parking lot of the City of Knowledge School and entered the foyer, a woman in a long coat (called in Arabic a *jilbab*), her hair completely hidden underneath a *hijab* (headscarf), greeted me. This woman was the principal of the school, and I asked her if it would be possible for me to study Arabic there. She smiled and said, "Why not?" I asked her if I needed to cover my hair and she said that I didn't have to but that it would be nice if I did. I ran across the street to a hair products store and asked the tall African American woman if they had any headscarves for sale. She produced a tiny, orange polyester scarf that barely covered my hair when I tightly knotted it under my chin. She grinned and told me that this scarf was meant to be worn to sleep in so that my hair would not be matted in the morning. It was all she had to offer, so I bought it and tied it on. When I returned to school I was politely told that my scarf was a bit small but my intentions were honorable. I was taken throughout the corridors of the school and introduced to the female teachers. Like the principal, they all wore long coats and ample scarves that covered their necks and gently draped across their chests. The next day I returned and was gifted numerous scarves. Later that week I purchased a long jilbab, and from then on I too was covered from head to toe like the other women there. I was placed in the fifth grade with twenty-five children, but a few weeks later I would be demoted to the third-grade Arabic class.

Just a few weeks after I started at the school, I was invited to attend the most important of the Shi'a rituals, Muharram. This series of rituals profoundly influences the identity construction of these Muslim women, and in turn, the women and their rituals strongly affected my heart. As I participated in their rituals, I too would weep, understanding the language of their tears.

I had entered what I fondly call the "Shi'a vortex." Over the next four years I studied and taught at the school, establishing friendships that led to invitations to weddings, baby showers, funerals, and religious rituals and events. Most important, I made friends with numerous families that consider themselves deeply committed Shi'a Muslims. By this they mean that they have returned to the fundamentals of Islam, a commitment to follow the precepts and practices of Imamiyyah or Ithna Ashari (Twelver Shi'a) as established over centuries in Iraq and Iran. The Ithna Ashari is the largest branch of Shi'ism. The Prophet Muhammad; his first cousin Ali; Fatima, the Prophet's daughter and wife of Ali; and Hassan and Husayn, the children of Fatima and Ali, comprise the *ahl al-bayt*, the people of the house, fondly called the holy family. I began to love the ahl al-bayt, the holy and beloved family of the Prophet Muhammad, and to understand the language of tears. These tears, wept on behalf of the holy family during their rituals, would bond me to the community and lead me to a long-term study of Shi'ism and how Shi'a Muslims live their lives, especially in the United States.

In 1994 the City of Knowledge School was founded by an Iraqi woman who was a practicing dentist. As her own children grew she became concerned about their participation in public schools, so she and a small group of Iraqis and Iranians started this small private school. Since the school opened she has obtained a PhD in education. The school building is an old bowling alley converted to classrooms, with a large multi-purpose room and a prayer hall where people and students meet to pray and study. There is a prayer room that is covered wall to wall with beautiful carpets. The majority of the students there are Shi'a, and their parents are from Iraq, Iran, and Pakistan. There are smaller groups from Lebanon, Syria, and even Saudi Arabia. Almost all the students from preschool through high school were born in the United States or came as very young children. As in any other school the halls are full of laughter and teasing, but in the classrooms, after children reach the age of nine or ten, boys sit on one side and the girls on the other.

When I entered the fifth grade as a fifty-year-old woman to study Arabic, the children thought I was hilarious. They asked me lots of questions. Once, when they saw my hair, a girl exclaimed, "You're a redhead! We thought you would be blonde!" Their enthusiasm that I would learn Arabic and convert to Islam was never stifled. They helped me in class, explained why there were certain requirements to follow, and taught me to pray. These ten-year-old girls took me under their collective wing to make sure that I was receiving a proper Islamic education. They told me not to worry; they would teach me *wudu*, the proper way to wash before I prayed, and they would teach me the prayers in Arabic and how to stand with other women in a row, shoulder to shoulder, side by side.

After my first week there I was invited to stay after school to participate in Muharram, the annual observance of special rituals, performed mostly by Shiʻa, to commemorate the martyrdom of the holy family. I would watch them beat their chests, shed tears of sorrow for the Prophet Muhammad's family, and commemorate and lament the past. Before long, I too would join in the rituals, weeping alongside them. These Shiʻa, unknown and misunderstood, are seen as a mysterious group by Muslims and non-Muslims alike. As the years went by, I would come to know their hopes and fears, hear what they felt were the benefits and disadvantages of living in the United States, and witness their sacred rituals. I participated in the ordinariness of their daily lives, their spiritual devotions, and ultimately a pilgrimage to Iran.

During my time at the school I would learn about the Prophet Muhammad; his beloved daughter Fatima; her husband, Imam Ali; and their children, all of whom play a crucial role in the development of Shiʻa theology. I would meet smitten young women excited to be married, mothers upset because their sons wanted tattoos, and refugees who wished they could go home. Still others were going to graduate school or working as doctors, architects, and professors. In the sexually segregated environment prescribed by their cultural and religious beliefs, I would spend much time solely with women, entering into their private environments.

My first friendship started with a woman who had invited me, at the request of her ten-year-old daughter, to her home for a women's gathering called a *majlis*. I was thrilled when I received the phone call from the girl's mother inviting me to their home to participate in a Muharram ritual. I had befriended this little girl in my

Arabic class, and she had asked her mother to invite me to this special ritual.

I was quite an oddity sitting in a class with children who were already reading and writing in Arabic. Little Fatima wanted to sit next to me in class and would whisper to me so that I might better understand Arabic. She told me that I must learn Arabic if I wanted to learn to pray.

The Qur'an was originally written in Arabic, and although it has been translated into every language imaginable, when it is recited in Arabic it has the most beautiful, melodic quality. People work hard to memorize and recite the Qur'an as beautifully as possible. This process and the musicality of the recitation should be *tajweed*, which means made beautiful, and should melt the hearts of the listeners. Fatima wanted me to hear and see, firsthand, why these rituals were so important to her and her family.

Although the population of the school was mainly Iraqi and Iranian, there were multiple ethnic groups, representing many parts of the world. As time passed I befriended numerous Iraqi and Iranian families. Later, I developed close friendships with Pakistani women. Of course, in the beginning I couldn't even recognize the difference in the cultures. Fortunately, everyone spoke English, and I relied heavily on the young women to translate. I was invited to attend gatherings in their homes and eat some of the most delicious foods ever.

Different people had come to the United States from Iran and Iraq for different reasons. Some of them were from wealthy families and came to the United States for an education, then decided to stay. Others were refugees who had been persecuted by Saddam Hussein or had experienced oppression simply because they were Shiʻa rather than members of the dominant Sunni sect of Islam. What binds them together is the fact that they are Shiʻa.

I met literally hundreds of women at lectures given at local masjids and centers. Women would sit next to me and translate what was being said. They sat close to me and whispered or handed me an English Qurʼan to follow. By the end of the four years that I spent with these women, I had been given a dozen head coverings and numerous books explaining Shiʻism. Some of these books were brought as gifts from as far away as Iran and Pakistan. I was also given the appropriate clothing to wear: a long black *chador* (the long, tent-like garment made from five yards of black fabric) from my Iranian friend Taibeh and from another friend, Masooma, two plain black *shalwar kameez* (traditional baggy pants and long tunic) sent from Pakistan. One of the most meaningful gifts was a *turbah*, a small, round piece of soil brought from Karbala, Iraq. (When the Shiʻa pray, they rest their foreheads on a molded, compact piece of pure, sacred soil rather than touch their foreheads to a dirty floor.) A *tasbeh*, a Muslim rosary, was brought to me as a gift from Iran. Years later I still cherish these gifts and the love behind them as I continue to participate in the annual rituals.

Over and over I was invited to Iran, Iraq, and Syria for what they called *ziyarat*. Ziyarat means visiting or making a pilgrimage and is especially popular with Shi'a who live far from Iran and Iraq, where the holy sites are located. In these two countries are housed the tombs of the holy family and their important followers. Every year millions of Shi'a make pilgrimages to these religious sites to pay their respects. At that time, I had no idea that someday I would make my own pilgrimage to these sacred shrines.

Although I had studied Islam, I did not feel particularly Muslim in the way these women did. As Twelver Shi'a, they had a much more conservative viewpoint than I did after studying Sufism for much of my life. Sufism is the mystical approach to Islam and shares many of the same dedications that Shi'ism does. Although my path in Islam was different from theirs, as a guest in their lives, I was deeply honored. I learned as much, if not more, about them from participating in their everyday lives and rites of passage than from simply being a researcher asking the same questions from a form required to acquire data for my research. As I worked at the school and studied Arabic, I became increasingly interested in Shi'ism and the women that I befriended. As time passed I gave up the idea of research in another country realizing that there was an immense amount of research that I could do on American Muslims in my own neighborhood. Not only was Shi'ism a fascinating topic, but it seemed that every woman I met had an amazing story to tell.

Participation in the rituals allowed me to enter into the community as an outsider but also as an insider. At one point I was asked to help wash the body of a deceased Iranian woman. In order to be allowed to wash the body of a Muslim, a person should be *mahram*, a relative, or at least be Muslim. The fact that I was asked to assist, when they knew I was not Muslim, was a tremendous honor. In this case, the women saw me as an insider, and I was granted privileges such as washing the body of a Muslim woman, when in reality I was an outsider. As an insider I had special privileges, but as an outsider I did too. At some of these special occasions I was introduced as "the one who is writing the book," so I was treated with respect. Everyone seemed to know who I was. This led me to believe that some of the people in the community had discussed my project and approved of it, hence the numerous invitations. At other times I was considered an outsider and felt excluded.

My feelings alternated between the two roles. I was not accepted by a family of sisters that held gatherings at their house every day. They were always very polite to me, but when I asked if I could interview them, all four of them gave me excuses, as did their daughters. One woman's husband had received death threats when they lived in Pakistan. They had come to the United States seeking asylum, so her fears may have been reasonable. I did not know this family from the Islamic school where I worked, so they had no reason to trust me; I had been invited to the majlis by a "friend of a friend." When I thanked them for inviting me, they said that I had not been invited but that the majlis was open to anyone who wanted to be there, comparing it to attending church where one is not invited but goes anyway. But clearly, in their eyes, my presence was a faux pas because I had been invited indirectly, through their friend. These situations, however, were rare. Over the four-year period, most of the women grew to trust and befriend me. I was told that initially the community thought that I was a government informant from the FBI. As a result, they avoided me or were very friendly, trying to prove to me that not all Muslims were terrorists. Initially, although polite, they were guarded. If the government could tap the phone conversations of millions of Americans, why wouldn't it use my research against them? This was a difficult question to answer; I couldn't promise anything. After all, there was a great deal of Islamophobia in the United States. Some of these women, especially those new to the United States, were afraid of prejudice and retribution after 9/11.

During the rituals, we wept as we lamented the deaths of the Prophet's family. But not all occasions were sad; once Muharram was over, there were plenty of celebrations, including engagement parties, weddings, and birthday parties. I would be invited to lavish weddings and very simple affairs. As in all communities there is a discrepancy in income. One wedding I attended was fit for a princess but another held at the school library lasted just a few minutes. This ceremony, as simple as it was, moved me tremendously. At seventeen a young Salvadoran woman had married an Iranian man she met in Los Angeles. She told me that she had loved him dearly, and after they had three children he had unexpectedly died of a heart attack. She had never wanted to remarry but now, seven years later, met a wonderful man. He was poor but good, she told me. There was a small group of us sitting in the library. Because her future husband was Mexican and couldn't speak Arabic, he had an interpreter. Within moments of the wedding he converted to Islam so that he could marry her. He uttered his *shahada*, bearing witness that there is no God but God, and then stated three times, "I marry you, I marry you, I marry you."

Also at the school I met a woman from Egypt who said she was Sunni but had married a Shi'a. Her daughter was pregnant and they were having a baby shower. "Please come," my friend insisted. "There will be lots of food and dancing." I had attended female-only dance parties and celebrations before and I knew that that they were really fun! Women came dressed in evening gowns covered in sequins and heavy gold jewelry. Even though it was a baby shower, by Western standards it would look more like a female-only cocktail party. "What will I wear?" I asked. "Don't worry," my friend answered. "I will find something covered in sequins for you to wear so that you don't look so drab." It had never occurred to me that, though publicly they were always shrouded in black or dark colors, in private their clothing was sexy and beautiful. In the private world, inside their homes, they dressed in all kinds of colorful clothing. I was the one that looked drab in my t-shirts, capris, and sandals.

Participating in their world was a gift whether it was a sad occasion like a funeral, or a baby shower where women wore sequined dresses and danced in the living room. I began to see the diversity of the various communities and of the individuals within them. Some loved living in the United States and some yearned to return to their countries of origin. Whatever their differences were, whether economic or cultural, they shared *tawalla*, the Shi'a commitment to express love for Allah and the Prophet Muhammad's holy family, the ahl al-bayt.

The people described in this book do not represent all American Shi'a. The families that I spent time with, for the most part, were very religious. As in every other religion, practitioners experience different levels of participation, allowing them to negotiate their religion so that it fits their personal needs. Individual interpretation is necessary for any religion to sustain itself. During my time in the community I met gay people that struggled with their sexuality and especially despaired of the relationship they had with religious dogma and the way homosexuality was viewed by the community. One woman was fine with the idea of her husband taking a second wife, but others insisted that they would demand a divorce. I knew couples that were happily married and women who said they were miserable. It was easy to assume that all the kids at school were religious, but really they were no different from any kids going to a private religious school: some were religious and some were not. Making assumptions about any group is easy to do until you spend a lot of time in the community and experience the diversity of individuals. As the years went by, I knew families where the mother and one daughter did not cover their hair but another daughter from the same family did. I befriended women whose husbands told them not to cover their hair, saying that they were making themselves targets in the United States and that besides, it was old-fashioned. These women refused to obey their husbands and continued to cover, arguing that it was their religious right and was between them and God. They were as diverse as any other group of Americans.

My goal is not to present an overly rosy image of Shi'a. I realize that as a community and as individuals they struggle with traditional cultural mores and American values. Balancing them is an individual response. I am aware that women in the community were pressured to behave in a certain way, as they would be in any institution or community. This book, however, describes my experience, which was overwhelmingly positive. It is true that they wanted me to convert. My conversion would bring *thawab*, or merit, to the entire community and prove to them that their religion was respected in the West. The women I interviewed wanted to be known and understood. The more I spent time with these women, the more curious I became. We started to develop a trust that comes from friendship and intimacy and from which mutuality, respect, and authentic affection between us flourished. I experienced a reciprocal tenderness, an appreciation for diversity, and the hope that, through a human connection such as ours, the world we live in will become a safer and more loving home to all her inhabitants.

The City Of Knowledge: Learning About Islam Through The Eyes Of Children

There are two directions in life, one is heaven and the other is hell, choose carefully the path you take.
SAYYED MUSTAFA AL-QAZWINI

When I started at the school I was put into the fifth-grade Arabic class. In exchange for studying Arabic I was supposed to tutor young children and teach journalism to teens. As it turned out I would learn more from them than they would from me. The children took great pride in teaching me about their religion. They were convinced that it was just a matter of time before I would convert, and when they asked me if I had converted and I responded no, they would smile and say, "Not yet." Believing that I had a lot to learn, they explained, translated, and coached me. The first thing I had to learn was how to say "Asalaamu alaykum" (May peace be upon you) and to respond with "Walaykum salaam" (May peace be upon you, too). This is the respectful way that Muslims greet each other. Initially it was impossible for me to memorize; finally, I wrote it on my hand and practiced reciting it as I walked up and down the halls of the school. I wanted to be respectful, and besides wearing appropriate clothing, this was the least I could do.

In many ways the school was just like any other. Muslim schools in the United States are developed around religious dogma and academics just like Christian schools. The principal of the school, a now-retired Iraqi dentist, had worried about the effect of American culture on her growing children and decided to start a nonprofit school in 1994. Today the school, named the City of Knowledge, has approximately 250 students, from preschool through twelfth grade, and has been fully accredited by Western Association of Schools and Colleges (WASC) since 2001. The vision of the school is to create an educational environment inspired by the highest ethical and moral standards of Islam. It offers summer programs for SAT preparation, and almost every graduating senior is accepted into a prestigious college or university.

The City of Knowledge School is situated in what was once a bowling alley. There are about twelve classrooms, a science lab, a cafeteria, an enormous playground, a computer room, a prayer hall, and a large space that can hold one thousand people for school plays, celebrations, and religious functions. Classrooms are decorated with the children's art and schoolwork. Each classroom has desks and chalkboards, and many of the rooms have carpets on the floors where children can sit for lessons or do their schoolwork. The cafeteria offers homemade food, prepared by mothers, that is *halal*. (Halal food for Muslims is similar to kosher food for Jews. Meat is ritually slaughtered after it is prayed over.) Volunteers and donations complete and sustain many of the projects at the school.

Initially I went to the school a few days a week to tutor, but I found myself so fascinated that I ended up going daily. I watched as the school library started with two bookshelves and within a year or two became a large room with thousands of purchased and donated books as well as films for all ages. Much of the furniture at the school was scavenged, secondhand, or donated. Knowledge was key to the environment, and learning was fun and interesting. I loved spending time with the fifth-grade students, who took turns sitting next to me and helping me with my Arabic and religion lessons. It was through them that I came to know their mothers and was able to participate not just at school but in their homes and respective communities. Because the children were predominantly Iraqi, Iranian, and Pakistani, I was privy to three different ethnic groups and cultures.

I started in the Arabic class; many of the other students were already fluent. They laughed at my pronunciation and the teacher chastised them. "Where is your kindness? Sister Bridget is trying to learn Arabic. It is your duty as Muslims to help her." Soon, I was attending classes with high school students. They were like any other all-American kids as they sat in class giggling, whispering, boys and girls flirting. Every one of them had a cell phone.

I was quite an oddity, sitting in a class with children who were already reading and writing Arabic. Many of them already spoke Farsi, Arabic, and English in addition to studying Spanish in school.

This first of the Five Pillars of Islam is *lā 'ilāha 'illā-llāhu muḥammadun rasūlu-llāh*, to bear witness that there is no God but God and that the Prophet Muhammad is the messenger of God. The second pillar is *salat*: one must pray five times a day. Before one prays he or she must perform wudu, which is a ritual ablution using running water. Muslims can pray anywhere; they do not have to be in a mosque. Muslims pray five times each day but I learned that the Shi'a actually combine the two afternoon prayers. For this, they receive criticism from Sunnis that they pray only three times daily, though Islam requires five daily prayers. In fact, the combined prayers are acceptable to Shi'a and they argue that the Prophet often combined his prayers.

One girl explained to me that the fast of Ramadan, also called *sawm*, would soon start. The fast, she explained, was the third pillar of Islam. I told them that they seemed too young to fast. When I asked at what age one starts to fast, she told me that girls start at nine and boys start at twelve but that you can start earlier if you want. Surprised, I asked why boys started later. "Duh," was the response, "everyone knows that girls are more mature than boys!" and they all laughed. If you are sick, menstruating, pregnant, or nursing, you are not obligated to fast, but most women still do. The purpose of the fast is to build compassion, and it should not be too rigid. Muslims refrain from consuming any food or drink, even water, from sunrise to sunset. One time at the school one of the boys uttered a mild cussword and was immediately chastised by the girls for breaking his fast. As a result, he would need to feed the poor or fast an extra day. At the end of Ramadan there is a great celebration called Eid al-Fitr. Everyone gets new clothes, children receive gifts, and there is a fabulous feast.

I learned that the fourth pillar of Islam is called *zakat*. Zakat is almsgiving. All Muslims, whether Shi'a or Sunni, are required to give a percentage of their accumulated wealth. In addition to this, Shi'a give *khums*, another twenty percent of all gains, to the Imams and the poor and needy. The fifth pillar is *hajj*, the once-in–a-lifetime journey to Mecca. One teacher told us that doing the Five Pillars was like having an insurance policy to eternal life. If you want to go to heaven, he said, get the best policy possible and generate as many good deeds as you can. He told us that Jesus brought people back to life not through magic but because of his connection with God.

One day I sat next to a beautiful girl who was fifteen years old. She introduced herself as Maryam. What a beautiful name, I said. She told me that she was named after Maryam, the mother of Isa. "Isa? Who is that?" I asked. She looked so surprised. "Isa is Jesus. You don't know who Jesus is?" I explained that I did but had no idea that Muslims named their children after the Virgin Mary. The girls told me that Maryam is the only woman in the Qur'an whose name is used. She went on to tell me that there is an entire chapter in the Qur'an about Mary and Jesus. "We love Jesus," she said. "He is another great prophet like the Prophet Muhammad." She continued to say that there were many prophets but that Muhammad was the final one. "Jews, Christians, and Muslims are all part of the Abrahamic lineage," she explained. "We are in the same family." "But why do you call God Allah?"

By now there were three or four girls around us and they looked aghast. "Allah is the Arabic word for God," she said. Honestly, I knew many of the answers to my own questions; I had studied Islam through Sufism and now at the university, but I was always curious to hear how Shiʻa would answer such questions. After all, I was there to learn from them.

Many of the students, and parents for that matter, were baffled that I was not Muslim. Are you Muslim? No. Are you married to a Muslim man? No? Why are you here? The entire community was patient with me. They couldn't believe that I had studied Islam for so long. Could I not see that Islam was the best religion? Well, I'm sort of Muslim. I follow the Sufi path; I'm just not as strict as you are. I was told, "No, no, Sister, the Sufis are crazy." I always answered, "That is what the Sunni say about you." "Ok, Sister," they answered. "As long as we are all Muslims, that is what matters."

I was told not to worry too much because my intentions were good, and that I had two angels guarding me. "One stays at each shoulder and records your deeds, good and bad, but they are not there to tattle to Allah. Don't be mistaken. They do know your sins but don't worry, the angels are on your side and they will whisper in your ear when you are bad, reminding you to be good. Just follow the straight path." This sort of religious conviction mixed with a sweet innocence warmed my heart. No one at the school seemed to be afraid that they would burn in hell for their sins. They seemed to take these religious beliefs in stride, accepting that we all make mistakes, we all sin, but Allah is most forgiving. After all, it is repeatedly stated in the Qur'an that God is most merciful and compassionate. I was told by young and old, whenever I did something wrong, that God would judge my *niyyat*, my intention, above all. "Don't worry, Sister," I was told, "you don't yet know our ways so Allah will forgive you. It is what is in your heart that counts, but just in case, you should cover your hair."

One of my favorite teachers at the school was Iranian. She was very pious, extraordinarily intelligent, and quite affectionate. This woman held a master's degree in biology and taught many of the science classes at the school. She was also in charge of teaching ethics to the high school students. I loved to listen to her lectures because they were truths from the heart—not canned, memorized speeches offered as a warning to those who sinned, a deterrent from being sent to hell. She had a great sense of humor and taught from the perspective that, as Muslims, students should be good for "goodness' sake." After all, what would make Allah more satisfied than a truly good human being following the ways of the Prophet himself?

During an ethics class she told a story of two women at Friday prayers. One woman was young and beautiful, a recent convert to Islam. The other one was old and pious. The old woman, born and raised a Muslim, knew the teachings of Islam perfectly. The young convert prayed piously and sincerely, from the depths of her heart, asking Allah to hear her prayers and accept them in his grace. As she bent over in prayer her feet peaked out from under her *abaya* (floor length coat) revealing bright red toenail polish! The old woman, seeing this, took great offense and chastised the girl, telling her that wearing toenail polish in the house of God was a terrible sin and that her prayers would not be heard! There I sat, with my own bright red polish on my toes. I curled them under my abaya, feeling like the wicked witch in *The Wizard of Oz*. The teacher asked the students, "Who is the better Muslim, which woman?" She went on to explain that one's niyyat, or intention, is what is most important. A greater sin is to judge another person like the old woman did.

I immediately went to the teacher after class and apologized for the times that I had worn nail polish during prayers. I was truly ashamed and had never meant to be disrespectful. She laughed and said, "Oh, Sister, you are just learning our ways, but now you know better." From that day on, I always wore black socks.

There were numerous times that the teachers seemed to get a big laugh when I did something religiously wrong or culturally inappropriate. They never scorned me; they thought that it was quite comical that I would do things that they should not. One such event was on International Day. Each class at the school represented a different country. My class, the fifth graders, chose India, and I had spent weeks making traditional Indian clothes for the kids to wear. I taught them a dance called *dandia*, which is done with sticks. The day of the performance, one of the students was out ill so I took his place in the line. As I was twirling and dancing, happy as could be, the teachers and other students clapped in unison. Suddenly a woman came to me and whispered, "Stop! Sayyed is coming and women should not dance in public!" She was referring to the oldest man at the school, a well-known imam from Iraq. This brought peals of laughter from the group. I was being naughty and everyone loved it. I was often granted special privileges like this because I was an American and essentially, from their perspective, didn't know any better.

Sayyed Mortada al-Qazwini, the man who interrupted my dancing, was indeed famous. Born in the holy city of Karbala in 1931, he was a major force behind the school as well as the Shiʻa movement in this country. Exiled from Iraq under the regime of Saddam Hussein, he ended up in the United States. When President Bush bombed Iraq, Imam Qazwini was immediately on a plane back to Karbala. His life was nearly taken when he was shot in an assassination attempt. My main memory of him is that he always yelled, "Yallah, Yallah" (Let's go, let's go!) just before the prayers or *hutba* (sermon) was about to commence. He seemed gruff and had no time for folly; he was here to save humanity.

Through the years I would learn that Imam Qazwini was deeply loved by all Shiʻa around the world. When I told people that I had been to the homes of his sons many times, they told me that I had been specially blessed by God to know this family. Among his five boys is Moustafa Qazwini, a very handsome and eloquent man who gave lectures at the school. He is the founder and director of the Islamic Educational Center of Orange County, as well as of the county's first Shiʻa mosque. I was fortunate enough to befriend his wife and the wives of his brothers, attending gatherings in their homes.

Sayyed is an honorary title for descendants of the Prophet Muhammad, and it seemed as though everyone in the community tried to claim this. Moustafa al-Qazwini was clearly a scholar and truly a sayyed. He held numerous degrees and his speeches were well organized and inspiring. His delivery went straight to my heart and his appreciation of a mystical perspective on Islam was in agreement with mine. On one of his visits to the City of Knowledge School, Sayyed Moustafa spoke about the importance of *du'as*. Du'as, extra prayers that are done in addition to the five daily prayers recited by all Muslims, are prayers petitioning God for something or as an opportunity to express gratitude to God. Sayyed Moustafa told us, "Never push yourself to recite du'as; only use the heart. You must feel the prayer in your heart." He encouraged us to take refuge in God and said that angels would protect us. We were told to research the religion. "You must know the truth yourself, not believe what others tell you." We were told that as Muslims we were responsible for all our actions. There was no scapegoat, no one to blame. "Your actions are who you become," he said. "They define your personality and influence others as well." He then explained that the Prophet Muhammad was sent to heal the souls of people and to help them with *akhlaq*, the medicine of the soul. This medicine is defined as politeness, actions, and reverence, and awe of Allah. He described akhlaq as a noble study, a sacred science that builds character. He added that in every step we take toward the mosque and whenever we make du'a, we should take into account our relationship with God.

At one lecture, when parents were present, he asked how many people had read the Bible. Only a few hands went up. "Shame on you!" he said. "How can we expect to know others and live in peace if we have not even read their holy book?" He then went on to say that Imam Husayn fought to end oppression not just for his followers but for all humanity. It was a spiritual fight for Christians and Jews too. The message from Imam Husayn is that all people have the right to live under Allah's banner. They have the right to express themselves religiously. During this particular lecture he reminded us that each step must be a conscious one, especially if we are on our way to pray. One's niyyat is the most important aspect of being Muslim. He added that seeking knowledge is, in itself, an act of worship. "Angels of Allah care for you continuously," he said. "They seek forgiveness for you. Allah will not reject the request of an angel." The young sayyed was extremely articulate. His voice had a lovely, soothing quality and there was no "fire and brimstone" quality to his lectures. He opened a book and read in Arabic, then translated into English: "Imam Ali says in the *hadith*: 'Avarice is disgrace; cowardice is a defect; poverty often disables an intelligent man from arguing his case; a poor man is a stranger in his own town; misfortune and helplessness are calamities; patience is a kind of bravery; to sever attachments with the wicked world is the greatest wealth; piety is the best weapon of defense.'"

The hadith are the second most informative texts, next to the Holy Qur'an, and there are Shi'a and Sunni hadith. The Qur'an was revealed to the Prophet Muhammad through the Angel Jibril, or Gabriel, as he is called in English. The Qur'an is the word of God and can't be changed, but the hadith are the sayings and actions of the Prophet; therefore, they can be interpreted from multiple perspectives. For example, the Qur'an says that one must pray five times each day, but the hadith explain how to do the prayers. Muslim women sometimes argue that the Qur'an gives specific and equal rights to women and that later, after the death of the Prophet, some of the hadith challenged or diminished those. I would later learn, when I spent time with young Shi'a women, that they believed the Prophet Muhammad to be the first feminist.

One spring I was invited to a birthday party for one of the girls in the third-grade class. It was held at a local park. The kids ran around playing while the mothers sat in one area visiting and the dads sat in another close by. By now, I was accustomed to the relaxed segregation of these age and gender groups. The party lasted for just over six hours, about four hours longer than most traditional American birthday parties. We feasted on grilled chicken, kebabs, hamburgers, multiple salads, and traditional American birthday cake. People seemed to eat in rounds. Every hour we would get up and help ourselves to more food. The day passed with much idle chatter. "Has anyone been to the new IKEA store?" "Did you know that Layla's daughter was accepted to medical school?" Someone complained about the price of braces for her daughter. "What next?" she asked. Her friend responded, "A dermatologist, a nose job, and a therapist!" Everyone howled with laughter.

Somehow the subject turned to *jinn*. Jinn are creatures made from a smokeless fire; as the Qur'an states, these little sprites can be believers or nonbelievers, but whatever their religious convictions, they can cause trouble. They are blamed for causing illness, preventing pregnancy, and all sorts of mischievous deeds. As we sat on blankets under the shade of a huge tree, I posed the question to the women: "Do you really believe in them?" One woman said, "Of course not; this is a superstitious old-fashioned belief." Another woman argued, "It is true, there are jinn." Her grandmother had a perfectly healthy baby that mysteriously died in the night and was convinced that it was a jinn stealing her baby's soul. Everyone offered condolences but a gentle argument pursued. One woman, a pediatrician, argued that historically people couldn't explain disease, so they blamed things on Shaytan (the devil) and jinn but attributed healing to the prophets and God. This may be true, argued another woman, but then why are jinn written about in the Qur'an? In the end nothing was definitively decided. As we sat there men started pulling out carpets to turn toward Mecca to pray. "Are we going to pray?" I asked. The answer was an emphatic no, only the men would pray in public; the women could pray later in the privacy of their own homes.

Men walked to their cars and pulled out small prayer rugs, took them under a tree and placed them for prayer. Someone made *adhan*, the call to prayer, and they started to assemble in lines. As I turned to watch them I saw that they were facing a group of young people dressed in Biblical costumes. There were the Virgin Mary holding a baby doll wrapped in a blanket, Joseph, and some shepherds holding staffs. The rest of the crew I couldn't identify. It was a group of Christian students practicing for the Easter passion play. There I sat in Southern California, watching two distinct religious groups offering their commitment to God. It was one of the most amazing sights I have ever seen. God bless America, I thought to myself!

The little birthday girl received a pile of presents. I gave her a ballet costume. She received jewelry, clothes, and toys, but her favorite present was Fulla, a Muslim Barbie doll. Fulla looked like every other Barbie doll. She had a purse, high heel shoes, a sparkly evening gown, and racy red lace bra and panties. But this doll also came with a head scarf and black abaya. Fulla could be as sexy as she wanted at home, but in public she would be appropriately dressed in modest Muslim garb.

Back to school we went on Monday, and I was told that the students would start preparing for the annual hajj play. Going on hajj is one of the Five Pillars of Islam and a once-in-a-lifetime requirement. Wealthy people do it more than once. It is the final dream and responsibility of all Muslims. As part of their studies the students in all grades are taught the importance of hajj; they are encouraged to start saving money so that some day they can afford to go. Traveling to Mecca, in Saudi Arabia, is very expensive: from the United States prices range from six thousand to thirty thousand dollars.

The kids were really excited about the parts they would get and began practicing memorized monologues. They rehearsed daily, and the older students constructed sets, including a replica of the Kaaba, the sacred monument in Mecca.

It was at the Kaaba that the Prophet Muhammad broke over three hundred idols that were housed inside, claiming, "La ilaha illallah!" (There is no God but God!) This is one of the most important utterances of all Muslims. The students had found old crutches, a wheelchair, and various other devices to represent the millions of people that make the journey every year. One boy had made a beard from cotton balls to represent the final journey of an old believer. The students reenacted the journey by walking around the gigantic cardboard box made into the Kaaba. It was painted black and covered in glittering, gold inscriptions from the Qur'an. As a group they walked around the monument seven times, as is prescribed. The use of canes and wheelchairs, and children helping older, disabled partners were meant to show that everyone would help everyone in the journey. Dressed in the traditional white cloth called *ihram*, made especially for the occasion, they circumambulated the great symbol. The ihram expresses equality of all people, rich and poor, and that there is no difference between them, prince and pauper. In the eyes of God we are all equal. The kids even depicted the waters of Zamzam, where Hagar, after being cast into the parching desert with her infant son, Ismail, found water, a testament to her faith in God.

As I sat and watched the kids act out the story, my heart melted. It reminded me of the times I had watched my own children in school plays, and the seriousness and the joy that went into the actor's commitments. The students at the City of Knowledge were proud of their accomplishments, and so were their teachers and parents.

In true Shi'a fashion we all cried, but today there was no lament, just tears of joy. At the end of the hajj play we shared a great meal and the beginning of a four-day celebration called Eid al-Adha. Eid al-Adha, the festival of the sacrifice culminates the end of the hajj. Every pilgrim has a lamb sacrificed and it is given to feed the poor.

It was in this loving environment that I made friends with the children's mothers. They would ultimately trust me and invite me to their homes for parties, weddings, Qur'an studies, and spiritual gatherings. I would record their stories and watch their children grow up. I would be allowed to participate in their gatherings and understand the spiritual and emotional cleansing nature of their religious rituals. Ultimately, I would see how the rituals and spiritual role models helped them in their daily lives by giving them strength in difficult times.

FATIMA: Lady of Heaven

As for my daughter, Fāṭima, she is the mistress of the women of the worlds, those that were and those that are to come, and she is part of me. She is the human houri who when she enters her prayer chamber before God, exalted be He, her light shines to the angels of heaven as the stars shine to the inhabitants of the earth.

THE PROPHET MUHAMMAD

While in the fifth-grade Arabic class, I sat next to an Iranian girl named Fatima. (There were numerous girls in the class with the same name.) Fatima took kindly to me immediately and invited me stay after school for a gathering of the women in the community. She told me that she was named after Fatima al-Zahra, the radiant one, the only surviving daughter of the Prophet Muhammad.

As the years went by, I learned that Fatima was one of the two most popular namesakes in the community, along with Zaynab, her daughter, granddaughter of the Prophet. I was given numerous books to read about

Fatima. The women were thrilled that I was fascinated by her importance. One dear friend brought me a book from Iran, which I read passionately through the night. Here was a holy woman who profoundly affected the lives of Shiʻa women. She held the same sacred space as the Virgin Mary does for Christians and Muslims.

Islam does not allow images. There are no statues or relics because the Prophet did not want people to make a God-like image of him. The Prophet Muhammad insisted that there is no God but God, so images would only confuse people, leading them to worship an image of God rather than God himself. As a result of this, there are no images of Fatima. She must therefore be imagined within the mental landscape of each individual who embraces her, creating a unique image that is deeply personal.

Her beauty lies in how her qualities are emulated and achieved by the one who loves her. In return she will love the believer as much. One of the women told me that Fatima has a scroll that is seventy yards long, and on it are all the names of the pious believers. Fatima will stand at the gates of heaven, and if you have been a believer your forehead will be stamped "believer." If you are not a lover of Fatima, you will be stamped "sinner." But no matter how many mistakes you have made in life, if you have loved Fatima and her family, she will stamp your forehead with "lover" and intercede on your behalf, asking God to allow you into heaven.

Lady Fatima is most beloved by all Shiʻa. As the daughter of the Prophet and the wife of his beloved first cousin Ali, she becomes the mother of the holy Imamate that forms Shiʻism. Known as the Queen of Heaven,

Fatima is the ultimate role model for women and girls. Her daughter Zaynab is also emulated by young college women because of her bravery and as a modern-day role model of a feminist who stands against her oppressors.

Fatima was the youngest daughter of the Prophet and his first wife, Khadija. Throughout history she has been idealized as the perfect woman, free from sin, much as the Virgin Mary is to Catholics. She too is seen as a pure and spotless being, the mother of a savior and martyr. Fatima died just a few months after her father, leaving behind her husband, Ali, and four children, two of whom are the famous and beloved Imam Hassan and Imam Husayn. These five people—Muhammad, Fatima, Ali, Hassan, and Husayn—are known as the ahl al-bayt, the people of the house, holding a very reverent place in the hearts of Shi'a.

Every day during Muharram, I heard stories about Fatima and her children. There are special du'as, prayers, for Fatima and her family. She is admired for her piety, her closeness to the Prophet Muhammad, and her intimate relationship with God. It is not unusual for women to pray to Fatima the same way Catholics pray to the Virgin Mary, if they are in need of intercession. If a woman is unable to get pregnant, if she has a sick relative or a death in her family, she will ask Fatima to approach God on her behalf. They often spoke about her as if she were in the room; many women believed that she was present at every gathering.

One woman told me that she was unable to get pregnant for many years, but when she started to ask Lady Fatima for assistance, things started to change. She laughed as she told me: "Fatima al-Zahra, may peace be upon her, must have listened to my prayers, because now I have five children. Now I pray that I won't have more!" We all laughed when we heard this and agreed, with good humor, to be careful what we pray for.

Shi'a believe that Fatima was born from light when God created the cosmos. She appears as light when people pray and fast from the depths of their hearts to end suffering, when they desire an intimate relationship with Allah. After the Prophet Muhammad spent forty nights fasting, meditating, and praying in solitude, he went home to his beloved wife Khadija. He had been instructed by the Angel Jibril to wait to pray, to see his beloved wife before anything else. Fatima was conceived from this heavenly union. The story details that among other saintly women, the Virgin Mary was present as midwife to Khadija during Fatima's birth. One hadith states that "indeed, on the night during which I was taken to the sky, I entered Heaven and I stood by its most beautiful tree, with the whitest leaves, and the most delicious fruit. So I took from its fruit and ate . . . and when I descended to the earth, I approached Khadija; and she became pregnant with Fatima from that produce."[1]

These sayings, recited for centuries, cement the relationship of Fatima to her followers. Because images are not allowed in Islam, the images of her kindness, compassion, and beauty are held in the hearts of Shi'a women.

---

1. Mostafa Hosayni, *Sayyedat Nesa Al-Alamen: Chief of the Women of the World* (England: Islamic Propagation Center, 2003), p. 25.

Little is known about Fatima's childhood, but she was married young, as were most women during that time. The life expectancy was much shorter than it is today, so girls married young, as early as nine years old, though they stayed home with their parents until their first menstruation, then moved to their husband's home to become wives and mothers. According to the stories, numerous men asked Fatima's father for her hand in marriage. He refused them all until his cousin Ali asked to betroth Fatima. From the Prophet's perspective, this was a marriage made in heaven! This physical and spiritual marriage would lead to a family of people that would have a profound effect on Islam and Muslims around the world.

One night, while sitting with a group of women and girls, we were served tea and offered cake. As we settled in, someone started talking about her cousin getting married. An older woman said that we should all be like Fatima and have a modest wedding. She then told us a story about a woman who was so poor she had no wedding dress. When Fatima heard this, she offered her own dress to the woman and chose to wear plain linen. The old woman said that as a result of Fatima's generosity, she was invited by God to experience everlasting life in heaven.

Our hostess told us that because of Fatima's piety, when she entered paradise, she was surrounded by angels and was adorned with a myriad of glittering, colorful lights and a crown covered in jewels. Just like the Virgin Mary, I thought to myself.

"You see," our hostess said, "God gave Fatima these robes of light as a heavenly wardrobe, placing her in a special role so that we can turn to her when we are in need. Her holiness is marked by her kindness and generosity, and as women, we want to be the same kind of brides, wives, and mothers. If we love her, we will be rewarded in heaven. She will see our tears and love us in return."

She continued to tell me that Fatima died shortly after the death of her father, and that her death is surrounded by controversy. There are numerous accounts of her death, but in the Shi'a community the following one is the most popular: Fatima, with child at the time, hid behind a door because she was home alone and unveiled. Her husband's enemies forced open the door, and she was impaled by a large nail. She was then pulled from behind the door and beaten repeatedly until she miscarried. Fatima died hunched over in prayer after giving birth to a stillborn child. Because Fatima was conceived in prayer and the last words she uttered were prayers, she is considered pure prayer. Fatima was granted the opportunity to meet her beloved father in paradise, leaving behind a husband and four children. For this reason, she is often seen as a martyr.

They told me that the Iraqis call her Maryam al-Kubra and the Iranians call her Hazrat Fatima or Fatima al-Zahra (the pure) and that she is the mediator between heaven and earth. She helps to guide believers on the right path to Islam, the path of love, charity, and piety. Shi'a women use her as a role model whether they are young virgins, wives, or mothers. Fatima is seen as a woman full of grace, a material being radiant with light. She and her entire family are considered particles of light sent by God to redeem humanity. A small Pakistani girl looked at me and said, "Mrs. Bridget, we call her Bibi Fatima and she is a mother to all of us."

The women's stories consistently uphold these beliefs because they believe that their prayers have been granted. One college student told me that she had been in trouble, wanting to drink and party, until the night she had a dream about Fatima. She described the dream as follows:

> In my dream Lady Fatima appeared. She stood there, with a slight smile on her face, and said nothing. She was radiant with light pouring from her body and swirling around her. I woke up and felt an incredible peace and infinite love. She didn't have to say anything. I knew what needed to be done. I began to ask myself, "Who am I? Why am I acting so crazy?" After this dream, my life changed. I became more serious about my religion, my goals, and my general attitude. I felt that if she could turn me around just by her silent manifestation of light, I needed to listen more carefully and to act more responsibly.

She added, I believe that Fatima embodies the qualities of wisdom and love. She is the movement of love. Through my devotion to and love of Fatima, I have learned to love. Fatima encompasses all that is the divine feminine. Through her suffering, humanity is redeemed. God sent the Prophet Muhammad as a gift to the people of the world and in return the Prophet gifted us with his daughter Fatima.

It seemed that everywhere I turned, Fatima was there to soothe the soul, give hope, and cultivate faith in the women who revered her. My Arabic teacher was one such woman. One of the happiest people I have ever met, she was always laughing and telling funny stories. Troubles, misfortunes, and worries seemed to roll off her; she never worried about anything. I asked the secret to her Buddha-like nature. She laughed and told me how her love for Fatima had given her strength throughout her entire life. Interestingly, her name was Salaam, which means "peace" in Arabic.

Salaam had worked as a teacher at a Catholic school in Lebanon before coming to the United States. When I asked her about Fatima, she told me that Fatima had appeared to her in a dream, giving her a sign to be more pious. In the dream, Fatima had given her important messages. Her description of her dream is as follows:

In my daily life I did not cover my hair, because I was working at a Catholic school. Then I had a dream about Fatima, who didn't talk to me but was holding a mirror in her hand and was looking at her face in the mirror, reciting a verse from the Qur'an. There was light shining from her face. I asked her a question, "Why are you beautiful like that?" and Lady Fatima said, "Because I am covering my hair and not showing myself, looking strange, and putting makeup on my face." She was really beautiful and so I thought, maybe she is telling me to cover my hair. The next day, I went to the Catholic school where I was working. The people there were very nice, and I loved them a lot, but I was afraid that I would lose my job for covering my hair. But I bought some scarves anyway.

Salaam said that her commitment to Fatima was so strong that when she went to work at the Catholic school the next day, she had decided to wear a scarf and to understand if they released her from her position. She explained to the priest that Fatima had come to her in a dream with a message from Maryam, the mother of Jesus, telling her to be pious, pure, and modest. The priest, principal of the school, told her that they wanted her to stay. He said that she had the right to observe her religious traditions, and that without Muslims there would be no school there in Lebanon.

Salaam related that she loved the school for many reasons, not just because the people there were wonderful, but that she loved Maryam as well. She told me that she had learned a lot from Maryam and Fatima. They were the most patient women in heaven and on earth. When Salaam heard the story of how Maryam saw her son Jesus die on the cross, she cried and cried. It reminded her of the story of Fatima, who was martyred and, also like Maryam, the mother of martyred sons. She said, "If I have learned anything from Fatima and Maryam, I learned how to be patient when something hard happens to me."

Salaam's life was full of sorrow but her faith kept her strong and happy. Shortly after Salaam was married and moved to the United States, her husband was in a serious car accident, which crippled him and left him in a wheelchair. Salaam then had two small daughters and a disabled husband to care for. As she emulated Fatima, she stayed strong and faithful to Islam. Because Fatima lost her mother and father early in life, she was the model of the pious spiritual woman.

One year after I befriended Salaam, she was diagnosed with breast cancer. All these trials in her life, and
she hadn't even reached the age of forty. When I asked
her how she made it through one struggle after another,
she always said that Fatima al-Zahra had given her faith,
hope, and perseverance. She referred to the story of
Fatima, who foresaw her own death and her children's
martyrdom yet remained faithful to Islam. Fatima never
gave up her faith that there was some meaning in the suffering that God presented her with. Some Shiʿa believe
that the members of the holy family foresaw their deaths
but fearlessly chose martyrdom in the same way that
Jesus did. Salaam told me that while he was dying, the
Prophet Muhammad whispered in Fatima's ear that she
would be the first to join him in paradise.

Salaam told me that Fatima had lost her life and the
life of her unborn child when she was attacked by men
who wanted to change Islam to allow drinking and de-
bauchery. Salaam related that Fatima kept asking God to
help her be strong and fight for Islam, and that it is this
message that goes to all the women in the Shiʿa community, so they wish to be like Fatima. She said that Fatima
has given her patience and hope, and this hope and faith
extend to all people all over the world.

Months later, I was invited to Bibi Fatima's birthday
party at a Pakistani center called Jafaria. Some of the
women knew that I was researching Fatima for my doctoral dissertation and asked me to be the guest speaker.
This was a "ladies only" party. I appeared in my usual
black garb that I wore to all the Shiʿa functions. When I
arrived I was amazed to see women beautifully dressed.

I was accustomed to a short speech, prayers, and rituals that usually involved vows and a few tears. Tonight was different from anything I had seen at a center before. Women were exquisitely dressed in saris and shalwar kameez, the traditional outfit of pants and a long tunic, covered in sequins, small jewels, and pearls. I felt I was drifting in a sea of jewels. The saying "God is beautiful and he loves beauty" instantly came to my mind. This evening was a complete contrast to the somber Muharram gatherings, where everyone wore black clothing with minimal makeup and jewelry. Not only was their clothing lavishly decorated but so were they. Arms were covered in gold bangle bracelets, and multiple necklaces laden with diamonds, rubies, and emeralds graced the necklines. Their earrings were bell-shaped domes hung with jewels that dangled and made twinkling sounds as the women laughed and bobbed their heads. Sisters wore matching outfits and had smaller replicas of the same jewels their mothers wore.

On Mother's Day, in an Iranian Jafaria masjid, Fatima is honored and roses are given to all the mothers in attendance. I attended one such event when there was a special ladies program; afterwards the men served food that they had prepared and passed out roses. There was singing and clapping, something atypical of what I had seen elsewhere. My image of the sorrowful, suffering Shi'a was being challenged; I could see that there were plenty of joyful celebrations in the community.

Throughout the year on Thursday nights, when most Shi'a communities meet, and on Fridays for *Jummah* prayers, Fatima is often mentioned. Sermons explain the importance of women in Islam with references not only to the women in the Prophet's family, such as his first wife, Khadija, but also to Maryam, the mother of Jesus. Women are encouraged to emulate these holy mothers, putting God and family first.

The more time I spent in the Shi'a community, the more fascinated I became with Fatima. I wanted to hear every story possible. One year I talked my son into coming to Southern California to make a documentary film about the Shi'a community. We attended a Muharram gathering at a Pakistani center and met a family that had eight children. Their mother was from Germany, their father from Pakistan. All the girls had long hair and chubby, rosy cheeks like their mother, and the boys were thin and dark like their dad. The boys had long, shoulder-length hair, and when I asked them why, they explained that all the prophets had long hair, so they imitated them. My son and I spent a fair amount of time with this family, as they were very friendly and jovial.

Like other Shi'a, these sisters had created their own *nowehs*, songs of lamentation for the holy family. In Pakistan and India there are guilds of singers, poets, and musicians that perform nowehs and compete for the beauty and emotional response that they receive from listeners. Women are not allowed to perform these publicly but do so in the women's section at the centers or in their homes. These rituals are based on a mutually understood speech between speaker and participant that includes political discourse along with moral messages that are shared and interpreted. Nowehs should elicit tears from the audience, and they always did. Members of the community spent a great deal of time practicing these lamentations and performing them.

The verses the German-Pakistani girls wrote were chanted in English, yet had the same lyrical quality that you would hear in the mother language. The sisters told me that they had created *nowehs* and put them on YouTube and on their family's website. They invited my son and me to meet them in a park for a peace demonstration against the war in Iraq. We sat on the grass and chatted about Fatima, and they offered to chant their lament for Fatima. It had the same lyrical quality that I heard other Pakistanis chant in Urdu, but it was in English! Their lament is as follows:

Daughter of Fatima, Daughter of Murtaza
Oh innocent and pure, Daughter of noor (holy light)
Helpless at the sight, of her brother's plight
Helpless at the sight, of her brother's plight
No words can describe the tears in her eyes,
the tears in her eyes . . .

Daughter of Fatima, Daughter of Murtaza
Oh innocent and pure, Daughter of noor
Brother Abbas, everything is lost
Brother Abbas, everything is lost
There, so many men, where was my lion then
Where was my lion then?

Daughter of Fatima, Daughter of Murtaza
Oh innocent and pure, Daughter of noor
Tears fall down like rain, none can bear this pain

Tears fall down like rain, none can bear this pain
Oh my Father, console my Mother,
Console my Mother . . .

Daughter of Fatima, Daughter of Murtaza
Oh innocent and pure, Daughter of noor,
Oh my Sajjad! my Master my Heart!
Oh my Sajjad! my Master my Heart!
Nine hundred pound chains, You bear infinite pains,
You bear infinite pains . . .

Daughter of Fatima, Daughter of Murtaza
Oh innocent and pure, Daughter of noor
Sakina, my Hope, our necks tied by rope
Sakina my Hope, our necks tied by rope
Your Father on that spear, the pain is too severe,
the pain is too severe . . .

Daughter of Fatima, Daughter of Murtaza
Oh innocent and pure, Daughter of noor
King of Kings Hussain, are we near the end?
King of Kings Hussain, are we near the end?
Oh Zainab my heart, it's only one part,
It's only one part . . .

The sisters took much pride in writing and reciting their nowehs in such poetic fashion. Their love for Fatima was more than evident as they spoke about her. One said, "She is our Lady and role model. She gives us strength and hope and we want to be like her, full of prayer and grace."

Sorrowful yet courageous, Fatima represents the divine feminine in the hearts of men as well. Lady

Fatima resisted oppression, promised justice at the gates of paradise, and represents all beings on the Day of Judgment. When tears are cried for her and her family, and supplications are made in her name, Fatima is present to alleviate eternal suffering.

Fatima al-Zahra is a role model for Shi'a Muslim women because she courageously represents resistance and justice as well as familial and community love. For the past fourteen hundred years and more recently, she has been admired and elevated, most importantly because she is considered to be "chosen among women . . . from this world, but not of it," to grant intercession for those who stand outside the gates of paradise, not fully forgiven for their crimes against God. Shi'a women find authority, agency, and empowerment, particularly in times of oppression, by modeling the behavior of Fatima.

The Shi'a Muslim women I befriended regard themselves as having consciously chosen the paths of Fatima and aspire to be good Muslim women, putting others first and themselves second. They make a commitment to a larger, more fundamental goodness that is based on the preservation of femininity, gender roles, and religious authority. These women would adamantly argue that they are not oppressed by their religion, but that they enjoy God-given rights as Muslim women. During one visit I made to a friend's house, my hostess stood up and walked to the bookcase. She took out a notebook and told me that she would read me a supplication in honor of Fatima. The book was old and well worn, and everything in it was hand-written. As she started to read the room fell silent.

Peace be with you, O you who were afflicted with trials by the One who created you. When he tested you, He found you to be patient under affliction. . . .

Peace be with you, O mistress of the women of the worlds. Peace be with you, O mother of the vindicators of humankind in argument. Peace be with you, O you who were wronged, you who were deprived of that to which you were entitled by right. . . .

God's blessings on the immaculate virgin, the truthful, the sinless, the pious, the unstained; the one who is pleasing to God and acceptable, the guiltless, the rightly guided, the one who was wronged; the one who was unjustly overpowered and disposed by force of that to which she was entitled; the one kept from her lawful inheritance, she whose ribs were broken; whose husband was wronged, whose son was slain; Fatima, daughter of your Prophet, O God, flesh of his flesh, inner most heart of his heart . . . Mistress of women, proclaimer of God's friends, ally of pity and asceticism, apple of Paradise and eternity. . . . You, O God, drew forth from her the light of the Imams.

We sat cloaked in our black chadors, sipping tea as one by one they explained to me why they loved Fatima. Some women dabbed tears from their eyes and one said to me, "Do you see, we love her so dearly, so when we think of her suffering we weep." A woman approached us with a large tray, offering us tea and samosas. As we sat and chatted, an old grandmother kept interrupting her in Urdu. Finally I asked, "What is she saying?" Everyone laughed. My hostess said, "She is insisting that we tell you about Lady Zaynab."

ZAYNAB: Young Women and Feminism

For every girl named Fatima there was one named Zaynab. Lady Zaynab represents different qualities than does her beloved mother, Fatima. As the granddaughter of the Prophet Muhammad, Zaynab was seen by the high school girls and college women as a strong feminist. As one woman said, "Lady Zaynab was a radical, outspoken feminist in her time. She was a bad ass!" These young women were like most other American teenage girls, interested in makeup, fashion, music, and boys. They complained that their brothers had more freedoms than they had and that their parents "guarded" them more. Yet they still had all the fun that other American girls their age experience. They went to the mall, traveled to exotic places like Lebanon, Iran, and Iraq, went snowboarding, and played soccer. Their parents emphatically trusted them and they deserved such trust. Some of them struggled with wearing the scarf, which music was appropriate, and what films were okay to watch. Most of them were very serious about going to college. These women had dreams of becoming doctors, attorneys, and architects, and one wanted to be a film producer. They were carving their way through unfamiliar territory as Muslim American women. Different from their mothers, they had strong opinions about everything from plastic surgery to whom they would choose to marry. Whether they were Iranian, Iraqi, or Pakistani, they were hip and cool, pious and punk. Interestingly, they seemed to have a much greater knowledge of politics than other young people their age, probably because they were directly affected by how the media portray Islam, the Middle East, and Muslim women.

Every year they continued to help out at the school and, during the month of Muharram, lead the gatherings in the same manner that their mothers and grandmothers had. Often they came late or left early because they had homework or exams, but they knew that the future of Islam was in their hearts and hands, which gave them a sense of responsibility for the rituals and gatherings. As women born in America to immigrant parents, they experienced fluid cultural values, moving from traditional roles assigned by their parents to American values and behaviors that they chose. These women, as hybrids, negotiated between two worlds. They typically referred to themselves as Americans, stressing the difference between themselves and their mothers. A number of young women said that their mothers' generation did not have the freedom of self-expression that they had. These young, American-born women argued that they embraced Islam because they had researched it, not because they blindly followed their parents. They embraced the histories of their mothers yet forged a new future for themselves, one that is both traditional and modern.

As a result of growing up in America, they viewed the world and their religion from a lens that differed from that of their mothers and grandmothers. This does not mean that they were less religious than their elders, but that they interpreted their religion somewhat differently. They believed that they could be modern and pious, traditional and feminist at the same time. These women used their religion to argue their rights.

As American-born Muslims they had different experiences than their mothers had. One young woman felt frustrated with her mother. Refugees from Iraq, they had lived in the United States for nearly twenty years. Her mother kept telling her, "As soon as you kids graduate from college we are going home." Half the children in the family were born in the United States. Finally, my young friend told her mother, "We are home. This is our home now!" She said that her mother burst into tears and then the daughter felt really guilty. She told me, "Although my mother dreams of going back, I can't imagine going to live in Iraq. I have never even been there. Sure, I'm an Arab, I'm Iraqi, but really, I'm an American. I can't imagine going to live there. It is my mother's home, not mine." This was a common story for refugees; they came to the United States because they had to, not by choice as immigrants do. During the years I lived in Nebraska I yearned to go home to California, and every chance I had I went back to visit. It is unimaginable to me that I could never go back. This gave me a very different and heartfelt attitude toward refugees. The girls that grew up in the United States didn't feel like refugees like their mothers; they felt at home here. By the time they were in college they were accustomed to having male friends, sitting next to boys in class, and working with people of the opposite gender. These girls, in most ways, were like all other "all-American" girls, as one said, "whatever that is." Her friend chimed in, "Blonde haired and blue eyed," as she wrinkled up her nose. Another girl replied with a smile, "Not anymore!" They all laughed out loud. We all knew that the American landscape was changing into a diverse and rich culture.

On one occasion, when the girls were still in high school, I took them to a movie. Some of them pulled off their scarves, saying that they didn't feel comfortable wearing them in public. Others left them on. There were differing ideas of whether hijab was mandatory. They had to wear scarves as part of their school uniform, but outside school they were pleased to make their own choices. Some parents allowed them to go without a scarf and others didn't. Some of their mothers wore scarves and others didn't.

In the car, however, religious rules were the least of their concerns. I had NPR playing on the car radio and one of the girls asked if she could change the station. I said, "Sure." Within seconds hip-hop lyrics were blaring out the windows of my little VW Beetle and the girls were dancing in their seats. I told them that I thought music was *haram* (forbidden) and they all laughed. "No," one said. "It's not haram; it is only forbidden if it's degrading to women. We like it as long as it doesn't say bitch and ho [whore]." One young woman insisted, "This is un-Islamic to speak about women in such a negative way. No one can speak of a woman in this way, and any Muslim musician that does is an ass!"

Some Muslims say that music is forbidden in Islam, but most strongly disagree. I knew that all the young women listened to music, but what kind? I had been told that only classical or meditative music was okay to listen to. Music with words or rhythms that suggested anything sexual was forbidden because it might lead people to sin. Of course, many of the young women listened to all kinds of music and rolled their eyes when I asked them if it was allowed. They responded that they could, in a sense, sift the fine from the coarse and were mature enough to choose and listen to a variety of tunes. After all, one said, "I know who I am spiritually; no music will change that." They listened to classical music and hip-hop by popular Muslim rappers like Mos Def, Native Deen, and 3ILM because they are hip, cool, Muslim and don't have any messages that degrade women. One young woman told me that some of the lyrics today were so disgusting and explicit that she didn't want that kind of trash entering her mind. She said that it had nothing to do with religion—it was just disgusting. Why would anyone want to hear a song about rape, violence, and murder? Most of these girls argued that music is generally not forbidden.

As we pulled onto the freeway I asked the girls to tell me about Lady Zaynab. One responded, "For us, Lady Zaynab embodies a revolutionary woman resisting Westernization and political and religious oppression. She carried a critical message against oppression and is outspoken about it. She had strength of mind, compassion, dedication to others, and the courage to speak. She stood, chained, her scarf torn off her hair, and basically told Yazid to go to hell." The girls explained to me that

Yazid was responsible for the murders of many of the Prophet's family members. As one of the only survivors Zaynab was brave enough to confront him. As a result of this story many modern women chose her as a role model because they too had suffered.

The girls reminded me that their mothers and grandmothers had lost husbands, brothers, and children over recent years in Iran and Iraq. They compared their losses to the grief that Zaynab suffered when her family was martyred. "Remember," one girl said, "Zaynab did not collapse but continued to bravely speak out against her oppressor." The suffering of their mothers and grandmothers had made those young women the Zaynabs of the future. Like Zaynab, they established a strong sense of self in response to the suffering they experienced when their sons, daughters, or husbands were martyred.

The young women put tremendous importance on the female role models that their mothers emulated. Like Fatima, her daughter Zaynab is an elevated and beloved role model, especially for young Shi'a women. The young women seemed to identify more with Zaynab because they saw her as a feminist, picking up where her mother Fatima left off. As a feminist, Zaynab offered much inspiration for young women in contemporary times. When it came to Zaynab, they insisted that she was the prototype for young women's courage and piety. Daughter of Ali and Fatima, granddaughter of the Prophet Muhammad, she maintains the image of a young woman who spoke her mind against all oppression and injustice, challenging her oppressors in the court of her father's murderer. Zaynab was a wife, mother, daughter, and sister, representing the needs and hopes of all women during their lifetimes. But more than that, Zaynab stood up against those who oppressed her and her family. She spoke her mind when traditionally women were supposed to be unseen and unheard. Her spiritual and political zeal encouraged these young women to be authentic individuals and stand up for their rights. Zaynab continues to be emulated by Shi'a Muslim women today and is a role model of piety and resistance, engaging the hearts of every Shi'a woman who fights against oppression. One young woman told me: "I love Zaynab because she stood up for Islam and she stood up for herself. In a time when women were supposedly seen and not heard, she confronted Yazid, condemning him for murdering her family and denigrating Islam."

Centuries ago, Zaynab became a symbol of courage, in particular for Shi'a women. She remains a symbol of courage for today's women in Shi'a communities who fight for the right to define freedom and agency within their own religious culture. Considered to be the protector of children and the mother of the house of the Prophet, Zaynab is seen as an exemplary mother, one of the most important roles assigned to Muslim women by Islam. She is considered a patron saint to mothers, orphans, and the oppressed. Regarded as the embodiment of purity, justice, kindness, generosity, faith, and hope, Zaynab holds the image as protector of orphaned children and widowed women, making her the only female saint referred to by the honorific al-Sayyida. One woman told me that Sayyida Zaynab is compared to images of light and perfume because these are substances that radiate and spread, filling the hearts of devotees with love for the ahl al-bayt. The perfume of Zaynab is so pervasive that when one takes a deep breath, the memory of her connects the person with the inner garden, where the dew on the rose petal is a form of *baraka* (grace). The qualities of light and perfume associated with her transport grace and illumination. When one prays to Zaynab as an intercessor, she appears as a divine mediator. In the majlis, women often sprinkle rosewater onto each other in her honor. Because of her bravery in the face of death, Zaynab is placed above many of the important male role models, as expressed in excerpts of the following elegy so commonly recited in Shi'a women's religious rituals on her behalf, written by S. Karimi in 1996.

Elegy of Virtuousness and Wisdom of Zaynab

Who is the preacher of the Qur'anic message?
Who is the guardian of children?
Zaynab, Daughter of Morteza (Ali)
Who is the most virtuous of all?
Zaynab, Daughter of Morteza (Ali)
The light of Ali, the loyal Zaynab
The pious one Zaynab
Courageous, patient, Zaynab is the light of Mostafa
(Prophet Muhammad)
Friend and helpful, the "King" of Karbala, Zaynab
Who is the pure light of God?
Who is the protector of orphans?
Zaynab, daughter of Morteza
Don't call her a woman, she is above man,
        she is more faithful than a man

Don't call her a woman,
  there is no one more courageous than Zaynab
Don't call her a woman,
  there is no one more knowledgeable than Zaynab
In her bravery and wisdom so similar
  to Haydar Safdar (Ali)
Who is the one with pious knowledge,
  the protector of women's interest?
Zaynab, daughter of Morteza
She shook up the city of Kufa with her pious
  Qur'anic sermons
With her patience she destroyed the
  kingdom of tyranny
Her enemies are worried about her now
She reinforced the legacy of her pious belief
Through the sacrificial blood of her relatives
Who is the heroine of the time?
Who is the shining moon?
Zaynab, daughter of Morteza.[1]

The elegy continues at length, describing the attributes that Zaynab exhibits in her protection of women and children. It also describes her ability to speak powerfully and eloquently on behalf of Islam and the ahl al-bayt. Many of the young women in the community have memorized this elegy and chant it at gatherings when they remember Lady Zaynab, as she is so fondly called. Considered the source of wisdom for all women, Zaynab

1. As cited by Faegheh Shirazi, "The Daughters of Karbala: Images of Women in Shi'i Popular Culture" in *The Women of Karbala*, edited by Kamran Scot Aghaie (Austin: University of Texas Press, 2005), pp. 109–110.

is called *Zinat*, the Jewel of Paradise, the light of God. In other elegies, Zaynab is also known as the remembrance of Fatima and is described as well spoken, knowledgeable, patient, brave, and virtuous and as the pride of both worlds, heaven and earth. Young women emulate her bravery and, even more, her faith in Islam. They trust the way that the religious and cultural rites of passage play in the decisions they ultimately make for themselves.

Today, women recall Zaynab to help them navigate modern issues that women face, especially sexism. When confronted with difficult situations, women examine their actions and ask themselves and each other: "What would Zaynab have done?" One woman, who holds a master's degree in business administration, says that she is reminded of Zaynab when she is in a difficult situation at work. Referring to Zaynab as Bibi Zaynab, the title used by Indians and Pakistanis, she says that she is able to maintain piety and still maneuver herself in a powerful manner in the male-dominated corporate world. She expressed to me that "when I'm sitting in a meeting, for example, in corporate America, I almost imagine myself to be in Yazid's court. Sometimes, I can make my point in a very strong way and it is Bibi Zaynab's strength that takes me there." Zaynab's strength is valuable to her, especially as she negotiates the American professional landscape, but Fatima's tenderness is, too.

One day, three of the girls asked me if I wanted to go to the local Middle Eastern restaurant for lunch. They knew I was interviewing women for my dissertation and they wanted to make sure I got their opinions as well as their mothers'. They were not nearly as guarded as their mothers; they wanted to be heard. We sat and started with an ordinary conversation: "The kebabs are good, but not as good as the one's my dad makes. Check out the waiter . . . he's hot!" After a hearty laugh from the group (yes, I agreed, the waiter was cute), I asked them if they considered themselves feminists. They unanimously agreed that they were feminists, but the kind of feminist was negotiable. They typically responded, "Of course I am a feminist. The Prophet Muhammad was the first feminist. He was the first to establish equal rights for women!" When their mothers were asked the same question they insisted, "Of course I am not a feminist. I am a Muslim!"

They had their own interpretation of feminism and strongly believed in equality of the sexes as a God-given right. Many of the women had a negative concept of Western feminism, internalized from media representations of feminists and feminism. These young women could recite from the Qur'an to argue their points. One reminded me of the rights of women when she told me that the Prophet Muhammad was the first feminist. She recited, "O mankind! Reverence your Guardian-Lord, Who created you from a single Person, created, of like nature, his mate, and from them twain scattered like seeds countless men and women" (4:1). She argued, "There is full equality for women in the Qur'an. You can hear it in the words 'of like nature.' In other words, women did not come from man's rib like in Christianity. Unfortunately some cultures have overlooked this with their ignorant and sexist notions and laws!"

For my dissertation I used the following definition of feminism as a basis for part of my thesis. Among other things, I argued that Shi'a women's religious experience, their beliefs, rituals, and community, established agency and religious authority, thus empowering them.

Feminism is a worldwide movement for the redefinition and redistribution of power. Feminism is: a) a belief that women universally face some form of oppression or exploitation; b) a commitment to uncover and understand what causes and sustains oppression, in all its forms; and c) a commitment to work individually and collectively in everyday life to end all forms of oppression. Given this definition, the ultimate goal of feminist research is the emancipation of women and the creation of a just world for everyone.[2]

This definition seemed perfect to me from an Islamic perspective and especially from a Shi'a one. The Shi'a consistently speak against oppression and argue that they will weep until the world becomes a just world for everyone. So I asked them, "If feminism is represented by the above definition, then all Muslims must be feminists, right?" One woman interviewed, who held a masters degree in Islamic studies, was adamant that she is a feminist, but "not in this way that Americans have picked up the term and applied it to women who don't shave their armpits; you know, that's not what feminism is about at all, or it's not about women being able to do men's jobs. It's about women being given the respect and the dignity that they deserve."

This young woman had a strong belief about what feminism is. She believed that women could be and do

2. Patricia Maguire, *Participatory Research: A Feminist Approach* (Amherst: University of Massachusetts Press, 1987), p. 79.

whatever they want. What they must strive for is respect for themselves and from the culture. She was a woman who worked, attended college, and was waiting to have children. I asked, "So what is the American definition of feminism?" She said, "I think, when I hear about feminism here in the United States, women and men should be doing the exact same things and whatever, and it's like, no, I think women and men are equal but there are different roles. Feminism is really standing up, Islamic feminism or whatever, is that women are recognized for their minds and for their intellect, and for what they have to say rather than for their physical assets."

They all agreed that feminism is about equality between the sexes but also about personal choice. If a woman chooses to be a stay-at-home mother she should be honored for doing so. This young woman suggested that women have many choices in life and a woman can be respected for multiple qualities. Her younger sister Hoda attended the University of California. Hoda had played on a hockey team and on a soccer team and was a skateboarder. She wore the most fashionable clothing and always wore hijab. She loved music but was selective about what she listened to. She had no trouble speaking her mind. I asked her the same question. "Do you consider yourself a feminist?" "Definitely," she replied. "I think Islam is such a feminist religion. First of all the Prophet married a woman who supported him. Second of all hijab is such a feminist concept. It says, ok don't look at me; look at who I am. It's such a feminist statement in itself. The religion is such a feminist religion for sure. Because American culture says you've got to always look pretty. A woman has to be representational of beauty in general, not a zit, not a mark, a flawless body. That is just what American culture teaches, while Islam says the complete opposite in regards to a woman's beauty: it should first be internal. Women of course have to be presentable and even beautiful, but you're not supposed to objectify yourself sexually."

Hoda spoke for a number of the women that were interviewed, in that she disliked the constant pressure on American women to be beautiful and sexy. She believed that women can have those qualities but should also be valued for their intellect and the ability to nurture and care for others. Neither she nor her sister felt that they had to be one or the other, a businesswoman or a stay-at-home mother. They saw themselves as having the ability to make different choices at different times of their lives.

The American-born women said that they had to think for themselves, whether it is about Islamic beliefs, American culture, or feminism. When I told Firouz, who had a bachelor's degree in Middle Eastern and African studies, that I was impressed at how articulate the American-born women were when asked about feminism, she replied, "I think that has a lot to do with your background and where you were raised. If you really think about it, back home or back in the Middle East or Southeast Asia, the women's opinion was never really appreciated or counted. I don't feel like their word had much worth or value. Nobody probably even bothered to ask them; they probably weren't asked certain questions or how they felt. They just kind of went with the flow and did what everybody did. They didn't really think for themselves, 'Why is it that I believe this, or why do I practice? We are Americans, it is different here.'"

Although these young women had questioned their roles, they typically conferred with their mothers when they spoke about women's roles as wives and mothers. There was a shared resistance to the Western construct of the "liberated woman" who is valued only through her thinness, beauty, and fashionable clothing. The young women created an identity through piety while being "modern" at the same time. Their identities seemed fluid, while they maintained a strong commitment to Islam, which provided them agency and authority. Their views on feminism also formed their beliefs about marriage. None of the women I interviewed had done much dating. Dating is not allowed in Islam, especially in these religiously conservative communities. Some had performed *nikkah*, an Islamic wedding in which a couple pledges to each other but do not necessarily consummate the marriage. They stated that they were married Islamically but would wait until they finished school to have a cultural wedding, which is usually quite elaborate. Most of the women that I interviewed were not married because they had decided to finish college first. They had career goals but insisted that being a mother outweighed a career. They all seemed to believe that they could have a career and be good mothers.

One day, I noticed that one of the young girls was absent from school. I mentioned that I had not seen her for quite a while. The girls all grimaced and then one rolled her eyes and said, "She's getting married." "What?" I responded. I knew this girl well. She was from Romania and had come to the United States as a very young child. Her parents had divorced and her mother had remarried. At fifteen, she rebelled against her family. She did not want a stepfather, so when a young man she was acquainted with proposed, she immediately agreed. The girls in her class were shocked that she was marrying so young. They told me that she was stupid, crazy, and throwing her life away. The guy she was marrying was ten years older, which they all agreed was way too old. "I can't believe her mother is letting her get married," one said. Another piped in, "Maybe they want to get rid of her." I wondered whether, like many parents who had headstrong daughters, they felt it was better to have a married daughter than a daughter who would possibly lose her virginity and never marry. This was a serious concern in the community. Many mothers were very afraid that American culture has too much open sex and because of this openness, combined with alcohol or drugs, their daughters were in constant danger. They watched them constantly and the girls never dated or attended mixed-gender parties or events. The young girls felt sorry for their friend. "Maybe she wants out of the house, but why not finish school?" they moaned. "Well, she is headstrong and will do what she wants; her parents probably can't control her." Her friends tried to make excuses for her. "After all," one said, "her real father was abroad."

A few days later, I was invited to the wedding. It was an amazing event, and I was invited to be in the hotel room with the bride and her immediate family of about twenty women. Most of them were dressed in what I would consider fairly sexy clothes. The bride was wearing a dress that was literally covered in layers of lace and rows of ruffles. There must have been twenty yards of fabric, and the veil cascaded almost to her knees. Much to my surprise the dress was fairly low cut, and she had hair piled high on her head, with rhinestones glued everywhere. At school her hair was always covered and she wore the boring uniform that all the others wore. I had never seen anyone with so much makeup on in my entire life. By American standards she looked like a prostitute, but as the years went by I realized that this is a common style in all the communities I participated in. She was almost unrecognizable to me. The rest of the family was dressed in cocktail dresses and very high heels. The young bride hugged and kissed me. She was thrilled that I was there and I felt really honored and complimented to be included.

As we went into the main ballroom of the hotel for the big event I was astonished. There were a couple hundred people present, the women wearing everything from extremely short miniskirts to floor-length abayas and completely covered hair. Most of the teachers from the school were there, and when I saw one I whispered, "It's rather heartbreaking to see such a young girl get married." She sighed and said, "Whatever Allah wills . . . but I agree. At least she is planning on finishing high school." Once the bride entered, the party started. There was a band and endless dancing. Men and women even held hands, forming a long line, and did a Romanian folk dance while the more conservative members of the community stood and watched. I was surprised to see such sexy clothing and then realized the stereotypes that I had acquired while working in such a religious community. What was expected at school was one thing, but the cultural customs still held tremendous importance. I realized that there are multiple ways of being Shi'a and being Muslim. It was wonderful to meet the groom's family and dance with everyone.

As I drove home I felt sad that she was marrying so young, but remembered another young woman who told me that her parents had "married her off" at sixteen to a thirty-six-year-old man from the "old country." He came to the United States to marry her and was allowed to become a citizen. Her story, which starts a bit sad, had an incredibly happy ending. She never blamed her parents for her miserable marriage but related that that was how it is done "back home" in Iraq. She said that now things are changing, but her parents were uneducated and terrified that when they moved to America as refugees, their daughter would be wrongly influenced by television, film, and American culture. They married her early to save her from the threat of American promiscuity.

I met with this young woman one day at a Middle Eastern restaurant and she told me her story. Four hours later I was amazed at her bravery, her passion, her forgiving attitude. She had decided to leave her marriage after having two children. One day, she packed her car, took the children, and ran away to Los Angeles. For a young woman from this community to leave against the will of her husband and family showed tremendous courage. When she arrived in Los Angeles, she said, she sought refuge with the Shi'a community. Although she said that she was not as religious as most of the community, they had taught her the true meaning of love and compassion. In a sense, her marriage had been forced, or at least arranged by her parents without her consent. This is very unusual in this community. Forced marriages are considered un-Islamic by most Muslims and are typically done outside educated communities. A forced marriage is usually the symptom of extreme poverty and desperation. There is a big difference between an arranged marriage and a forced one.

It was a sunny day and summer was approaching when some of the girls invited me to go with them to get pedicures. As we sat in a row, our feet being scrubbed, I asked the women how they felt about arranged marriage. I received a variety of answers. Sarah said, "If it's in the sense that the girl has no say, then I absolutely don't agree with that. But in the sense that the family finds someone who is also of a good family and they meet each other and they get to know each other, and they decide whether or not they want to be with each other, I think it's good because who knows better than . . . I mean, instead of getting some random person, you get someone with a good background and you know their family background and you know how they were raised. As long as you get to meet the guy and see if you're compatible and whether you want to do it or not, then I'm all for it."

Jasmine, a very outspoken eighteen-year-old, had a very different opinion. She had watched her mother struggle with a less than happy marriage with a man who was not a Muslim. She told me, "I feel that marriage should not be arranged. But if the person wants their marriage to be arranged and if they want their parents to choose their husband or their wife for them, then that is their choice. I believe that no choice should be mandatory and that you should be able to choose who you want to be with. I feel that if you as an individual want to choose who you want to marry, then you should have that choice."

All the young women felt comfortable with arranged marriages as long as they had a final choice in the arrangement. Although they were in agreement that they would never marry someone they didn't want, they said that they trusted their parent's judgment. In communities like this one, these women have very different choices than do poor women in places like rural Pakistan or Afghanistan. Without exception the women insisted that they would not allow a second wife. One student said, "You know, as a girl who grew up in America, I couldn't, I absolutely could not do it. You know, I wouldn't know how to. But there are people who are happy, and they do it and its fine. But that's just not the way I grew up understanding marriage. That was never my understanding of marriage. So, no, I would never do it; I would never ever do it."

A few of the women had parents that were divorced. They did not want to see themselves divorced like their parents but were adamant that they would never stay in an abusive marriage. Of course, most women have an idealistic view of marriage, whether they are Muslim or not. It would be interesting to interview these young women again in ten years. Life in America will afford them many benefits but also numerous challenges as they are influenced by the secular world. How do these women balance tradition and modernity?

The young women seemed to be able to laugh about their religion while staying pious at the same time. I guess they had to have a sense of humor, considering the way the American media was portraying Muslims as terrorists. One day, a group of us were working on a project when a young male student approached. "Hey, you hijabi jihadis," he joked.

He was referring to the fact that they wore scarves, hence the term *hijabi*, and that they were ready to wage a holy war. In the forty years I had studied Islam through a Sufi path, I had never heard jihad described as a holy war. Jihad simply refers to struggle; it is looking deep within and being self-reflective. There are two kinds: the greater jihad and the lesser jihad. The greater jihad is when one struggles against something that one's ego wants. As the male student walked away I asked the girls, what is your personal jihad? One told me that her greatest jihad was wearing a scarf. For her, wearing the scarf was most difficult. She said, "I wear hijab; that's probably my biggest jihad. I go out every day and people stare at me and people ask me questions and that's difficult. So that's a great jihad. And also, things like in school, graduate students are always going out and drinking and going to parties together and going to clubs together. You'd think they would be too busy because they are in graduate school, but every Thursday they go to a bar together and, you know, all the students do it. I'm the only one who never goes. And they're like, how come you never go?

And I feel like I make myself an outcast by not joining them in these social events because I know there's going to be alcohol and it's just not my kind of environment. So refraining from going to these things when I want to, when I want to be with my friends and hang out and stuff. That's jihad for me. I mean basically the way that Islam is set up it dictates a way of life."

A few years after I had finished my research, when I was working in another state, I returned to Southern California for a visit. I went with friends to a Middle Eastern café in an elegant neighborhood. As I entered I saw three women, two wearing scarves and one bare-headed and puffing on a hookah, a pipe that is used by men and women to smoke heavenly scented tobaccos. I watched them as they talked and laughed. The restaurant was filled mainly with white Americans in this college town, and the girls were noticeable. As I looked closer I realized that they were the young women I knew from the City of Knowledge School. When I went over to the table they jumped up and we exchanged kisses on each cheek. One of the girls was wearing jeans, a jean jacket covered in bling, high heels, and a headscarf. She looked really fabulous. The one with uncovered hair also had on jeans and a long-sleeved shirt but was wearing sandals. She looked like any college girl in town. Finally, Zaynab was wearing a long, elegant skirt with a blouse and matching scarf. She looked gorgeous. These were the same girls that during the month of Muharram dressed in long black gowns and chanted sacred elegies in honor of the martyrdom of the Prophet Muhammad's family. They participated fully with their grandmothers,

mothers, and aunties in rituals in which they wept and prayed, commemorating the martyrs and mothers of the martyrs. Living in the modern world they embraced an ancient spirituality that is part of their heritage.

We had a few minutes to visit before I was swept away by my other friends. They told me that they were all still in college, only one was married, and they were all applying for graduate school. They had maintained the focus and commitment to getting an education and still were very active in the religious community. After all, they were the next generation of Muslim women that would represent intelligence and piety, honoring their heritage as they moved through the modern world as contributors.

MUHARRAM

One Friday after Arabic class I went to the cafeteria with some of the young girls for the weekly treat of kebabs. Every week after Friday prayers, some of the dads came to cook deliciously spiced meat on long skewers that looked like swords. The girls were all wearing black and I asked them why. They explained to me that Muharram would soon start. They told me that they would start the annual grieving process for the Prophet's family.

That afternoon I stayed at the school and listened to the teacher tell the story of Imam Husayn and Karbala. This story is the epic tale of how the Shi'a were martyred trying to defend Islam. The teacher started telling us about the story of Karbala and how Imam Ali, the Prophet's cousin, tried to right the wrongs committed by other Muslims that were in power. Imam Ali argued that the government must be based on the Qur'an rather than on individual interpretations that some of the caliphs had promoted. This caused dissent in the community and a party of followers stayed on the side of Imam Ali, who by now was the fourth and rightfully guided caliph. Ali and his party were forced to leave Medina in Saudi

Arabia and go to Kufa in Iraq. Less than five years later Imam Ali would be murdered and his sons, Hassan and Husayn, would become the guiding lights of the Shi'a community.

Husayn and his followers returned to Kufa to restore Islam and oust the corrupt government of Yazid. They were refused entry into the city and were left on the plains of Karbala, where they had no water or provisions. Traveling with women and children, they suffered from hunger and dehydration. On Ashura, the tenth day of the month, after considerable battles with Yazid's forces, Imam Husayn was decapitated; his head was attached to a spear and he was paraded through the community. His family and followers were taken hostage and marched off to become slaves.

The teacher told the story as if it had happened yesterday. As she did, she started to weep. Some of the older girls cried but the young ones listened calmly. Later they explained to me that they had heard this story every year of their lives. As the teacher continued the story it became increasingly heartbreaking. As the story goes, children die of thirst and the women's headcovers are torn off, disgracing their modesty. A tiny baby is shot through the throat as he is held in his father's arms. Horses are killed or wounded and left to die. But the saddest part is when the Prophet's granddaughter Zaynab is paraded through the desert surrounded by all the surviving children who had just witnessed their parents being murdered. Clinging to her they desperately wailed. It was without a doubt the saddest story I had ever heard. Little did I know that, over the course of the next month, I would learn every detail about every member of the Prophet's holy family and Imam Ali's loyal followers. It was a story that would forever change my life.

The next day the girls asked me if I would stay after school for the majlis. A majlis is a gathering in which the participants sit and perform their rituals of sorrow as they commemorate the deaths of the holy family and their followers. These gatherings offer the participants an opportunity to lament the martyrdom of their ancestors. The young girls pulled on my clothes, begging me to attend. "You will be rewarded in heaven if you cry for Lady Fatima. Please come," they insisted. "You must come for *azadari.*" "What does that mean?" I asked. One girl curled her lip, looked thoughtful and said, "Well, I guess in English it means 'sorrow.'"

I followed the girls into the large prayer hall; it had been transformed into a completely different space. Usually we attended Friday prayers, classes, and lectures in the room but today the walls were covered in black fabric. There were banners covered in Arabic script, adorned with red and gold glitter. I sounded out the Arabic letters written on one of the banners, and to my surprise I exclaimed, "Ya Husayn!" (O Husayn!). I was thrilled that I could read Arabic, and everyone around me insisted that there was great meaning in the fact that I had read "Ya Husayn" before anything else in Arabic. "This is a sign from Allah," one girl said. "You are Shi'a! You are one of us!"

The majority of the participants at these gatherings were women whose children attended the school. Shortly after the school day ended, the gathering started with an hour-long lecture about some aspect of Shi'ism, particularly Muharram and the story of the ahl al-bayt. It was an opportunity for everyone to learn more and was especially geared toward newcomers and converts. The lectures were given in English for a handful of converts as well as for Arabic, Farsi, and Urdu speakers; the only language we all shared was English, so at the school that is what we spoke.

The small gatherings gave newcomers ample time to ask questions and were very informative. Local women who were considered scholars in the community led the gatherings. To be knowledgeable about one's religion was prestigious, and women spent plenty of time preparing.

I learned that the first ten days of Muharram are the most intense, when majlis are offered daily. From the first to the fifth days, the practitioners reenact the suffering of the family. There is particular attention paid to the laments of Sakineh, the young daughter of Imam Husayn who survived the ordeal. Each day another deceased member of the party is honored. On the seventh day the tiny baby Ali Asghar is honored, and on day eight Hazrat Abbas, the flag bearer who died while he was trying to fetch water for the women and children, is commemorated. Each day the sorrow regarding the deaths at Karbala are grieved until the tenth of Muharram, called Ashura, the day Imam Husayn was murdered. The grieving period ends on Arbaeen, the fortieth day after Imam Husayn's death.

As the afternoon progressed the room started to fill up with women dressed in long black abayas. They took their places in chairs against the walls or sat in a circle on the floor. As the room filled there were approximately

150 women present and it seemed as many children. There were very old Iraqi women with tattoos on their faces, barely visible through the very heavy folds of their wrinkled skin, and young women with nursing babies. These functions are segregated, so we were able to express grief privately.

Women started the ceremony by taking turns reciting and chanting elegies, the poetry of lament, in Arabic, Farsi, and occasionally English. Sung by one of the more pious women and recited with a specific rhythm, it is collectively responded to by the practitioners. After a few bars of the lament, the women started to beat their chests with either a closed fist or an open hand. This pounding was done with one or both hands, or participants alternated, with the right hand hitting the left upper chest and vice versa. As the participants became immersed in the grieving process they formed a circle and began, in unison, the rhythmic, ritual movements, stepping in unison, bending back, and then thrusting their heads toward the center of the circle. In unison they beat their chests and slapped their cheeks and foreheads, all the while chanting and crying out, "Ya Husayn!"

I stood to the side, gently beating my chest and watching their bodies bend back and forth, their heads thrown down, then back, hair flailing dramatically. I had never seen their hair before so was surprised that they uncovered for the ritual. One of the girls came to me and asked why I didn't participate in *matam*, chest beating. I explained that, although I wanted to, I did not want to disrespect anyone because I was an outsider. "Oh no," she exclaimed, "you must do azadari; you must try to cry

for the Prophet's family. Only then will you be one of us!"
She took my hand and pulled me into the center of the
room. "Sister, join us," she said. "Come and weep, show
your love for the ahl al-bayt."

I moved into the inner circle and started to take the
rhythmic steps, moving counterclockwise. I bent up and
down, hitting my chest and slapping my cheeks. I felt an
amazing shift of energy; it felt as if we were moving in one
continuous movement, completely synchronized. I felt
connected to every woman in the room, as though we had
become a sea of emotion, a movement in prayer. As the
rhythmic motions became faster, some women jumped up
and down, making staccato yelping sounds. One woman
stood in the center of the circle encouraging us to participate more fully. She made eye contact with one woman
at a time, intensifying her movements as encouragement.
It was as if she was supporting us to fully commit to the
experience. When she came to me I felt an emotional out-
burst, a tearful connection to her and the group. A number
of women *chasseed* (slid) back and forth within the circle,
barely avoiding a collision. At this point the energy in the
room felt intense, yet some women remain seated, rocking
back and forth while they watched, gently slapping their
thighs or chests. It was like two different movements in
a piece of music—one maintaining the rhythm and the
other improvising the melody. Suddenly, as if rehearsed, it
was over and we all sat down and started to weep.

A key element of the ritual was the weeping and wailing that came at the end. I watched as a young girl walked
through the room offering Kleenex. The women pulled
the upper folds of their black chadors over their heads

and held white Kleenex over their faces while they cried. For the women, weeping signifies a covenant: connecting them to Fatima and Imam Husayn, it ensures that when they die they will enter paradise.

After ten or fifteen minutes of crying, it was over, and then the entire process started again. This was repeated for about an hour and a half. Then women got up and attended to their children, who wandered around playing, seemingly unaffected by the sobs of their mothers. Tea and sweets were served and women spoke softly to each other. Bottled water was offered because, one woman explained to me, "it is important to drink water after heavy tears and also a reminder that during the Battle of Karbala many people suffered from dehydration."

Shi'a believe that the azadari ritual works as an intercessory prayer to members of the ahl al-bayt. All the members of the holy family, especially Ali and Husayn, are revered and were granted *shafa'a*, the power of intercession. Anyone who prays in their names is also granted shafa'a, for, as the Shi'a believe, Fatima, daughter of the Prophet Muhammad, descends from paradise to be present at each gathering. The prayers addressed to Lady Fatima and her daughter Zaynab will be graded in heaven on the Day of Judgment, and each person will receive credit or debit according to Allah's judgment. The women petition Imam Ali but focus frequently on the female members of the family as well, supporting their argument that Islam affords equal rights for women.

By internalizing the message of Ashura, women create agency and authority that is grounded in piety. They protest against oppression and injustice, and the tears they weep are considered to be spiritually and psychologically cleansing. Women's lives are made meaningful through participation in the azadari ritual as each woman gives voice to her religious convictions, and by commemorating the martyrdom of the Prophet's family, salvation is possible.

When the ritual was finished we sat and had a snack, drank water, and visited. I thanked everyone for translating and explaining the meaning of everything to me. After a few hours I was ready to go home and take a break from crying. I needed to eat, take a shower, and head back for the evening rituals. I was told that there would be many more people. They would come after work; entire families would come together and grieve. The cleric would give a special sermon explaining the importance of the rituals and why they should be reenacted. Though I was exhausted and wanted to go home, they wanted me to stay. I promised to return in a few hours and they said that I would receive rewards in heaven if I did.

I went home and cleaned up, then headed back to the school for the evening gathering. My car was in the shop, so I borrowed my daughter's bright blue Miata convertible to drive to the gathering. My black, billowing chador blew in the wind as I zipped past Blockbuster, McDonald's, and a shop that advertised X-rated films. The school had large black flags hanging from the flagpoles. As I drove into the parking lot full of every type of car, from a minivan to a Mercedes, I entered another world. A soft breeze circled my body as I tried to adjust my abaya and scarf. I was not accustomed to wearing such clothing and often tripped on the long folds of fabric, but as I entered the school that night, I left Los Angeles behind and stepped into a holy, consecrated space where I would sit and weep with other women about loss, sorrow, and injustice.

In the hall there were hundreds of shoes, all black, covering the floor. I removed my shoes, as everyone must do before entering the prayer hall, wondering if I would ever recognize mine upon leaving. As I went in, I was immediately greeted by dozens of women. I received two or three kisses on each cheek, as is the custom. Was I Iranian? Was I married to an Iranian? Was I Shi'a? When I answered no to all the questions, the women seemed baffled. I explained that I was working at the school and the children had invited me to attend.

The evening majlis was very different from the one in the afternoon. There were hundreds of people there, men, women, and children. People pushed their elderly parents in wheelchairs or walked slowly, arm in arm. Babies were brought in, held in their mother's arms, and fathers carried a child in each arm. Interestingly, although this was a time for sorrow and sadness, it was impossible not to see friends and happily visit. As the years went by, Muharram would be a time for me to connect with people I rarely saw outside the ritual environment.

In the huge room, men and women sat separately. In the Shi'a community at the school, the women sit and pray behind the men. At one end of the room was a large chair set on a platform. Here the imam would sit and give his sermon. These sermons were in English, Farsi, and Arabic. The imam is like a priest or minister; the role of the imam in the United States has changed greatly to meet

the needs of the modern American lifestyles of the immigrant populations. Young people, even if their parents
have old-fashioned values, grow up in the United States
with different concerns than their parents dealt with in the
"old country." The new imam must address these issues
and work as a bridge between young and old as well as be
a spiritual director for the community. I would eventually
befriend some of these imams and their families.

That night we prayed for the holy family but also for
everyone in Iraq that was suffering due to the bombing
the day before. The imam explained the importance of the
process of the azadari rituals and why we should remember the past and fight against all forms of oppression in
the future. He described the rituals' basis in love, saying,
"The love that the azadari ritual evokes for the ahl al-bayt
is described as the kind of love a person feels when under
the trance of romantic love between a man and woman.
The experience of romantic love is so intense and all-
consuming that all one's thoughts are directed toward the
beloved person. The end of that relationship becomes tremendously painful." In the azadari ritual, that intensity of
love is emotionally focused on the holy family, creating an
experience of ecstasy that no physical pain can penetrate
or deter. The sense of sorrow that accompanies that love
is focused on the suffering of the ahl al-bayt and the loss
of their lives. This notion was packed with emotion, and
after hearing this explanation I could better understand
the sincerity of the grieving and lamenting rituals.

Ultimately, although the rituals are supposed to address the historical suffering of the family and believers,
they evoke emotion over current situations, whether the

bombing of Iraq or the loss of a loved one. In a way, the ritual allows for the psychological cleansing of one's emotional state through a cathartic experience that is very immediate. This response to grief allows participants to acknowledge human suffering in a collective venue that differs greatly from the Western experience of grieving, which is primarily alone or in small family groups. I thought of my own grief process over the little sorrows in life, such as a divorce or death, and realized that I did much of my grieving alone, curled up in a flannel nightgown, tucked under warm, cuddly blankets, or with a paid therapist. This was in stark contrast to the community grieving I watched men and women express. Of course some of this grieving is theatrical and expected by the community to prove piety, but most of my experience was that the grieving process was very sincere. I was amazed at the way I became personally swept up in a downpour of my own tears when I heard the heartbreaking stories of suffering. Even years after I had left the school I couldn't discuss Muharram and the stories of Karbala without bursting into tears. Although I believe that, with time, all stories become more embellished, there was great truth in the acknowledgement of human suffering.

Again, I watched as the men stood and beat their chests and wept. Their faces buried in their hands, they cried for the holy family. They rocked back and forth as they sat cross-legged on the floor, which was covered with dozens of large carpets from the Middle East. As the men beat their chests, the rhythm of the elegies kept the entire group moving in unison. All the men wore black, and they often moved like a wave. The younger ones were more aggressive in their chest pounding; some of the older men just stood and gently tapped their chests. Sometimes they would move into a circle. What was particularly interesting to me was that the women sat in the background and watched, gently tapping their own chests or knees. They had nowhere near the energy that they expressed when they were alone and out of the male gaze. Women could watch the men but not the other way around. This challenged the stereotype that women are kept away from men for their own protection. Here women had the freedom to enter into both arenas but the men were not afforded the same privilege.

After the ritual was finished we then sat down for a meal of blessed food called *nazr*. The term n*azr* means "an offering" and, when referring to food, it means that the food is ritually prepared, by which I mean that it is prayed over when it is cooked. There were long tables set in a row, covered with food. Across the room was the same thing. I watched as men went to one side and women to the other, filling their plates. Although segregation of the sexes is the norm, if the women's side needed more rice, we went to the men's side to get it.

Some wealthy families have the food catered; it is considered an honor to host the event. Feeding everyone brings *thawab*, or merit, to the family that caters it. Many nights, however, it was potluck-style and there were ample portions of Pakistani, Arab, and Persian foods, a true feast for anyone.

Sometimes the gatherings would last until one in the morning. When they ended, everyone was exhausted from the crying and there was a deliberate quiet in the room as people pulled their scarves over their heads and bundled up small children who had long been asleep. There were hugs and kisses goodnight as everyone departed. If it was too late to sit and share a meal, participants were given food to take home.

These gatherings are extremely emotional. On the first day of Muharram, the first gathering I ever attended, George Bush bombed Iraq. The sobbing and wailing was very intense because many of the participants, being from Iraq, still had family there. It was impossible for me not to join in the crying. One girl explained to me that her mother and grandmother believe that the Shi'a have always suffered. From their perspective Saddam Hussein was the current oppressor, and now with the Americans bombing, things would get even worse. Unfortunately, they were correct. Things became considerably worse for many Iraqis, Shi'a or not.

I agreed with their premise that as long as there is suffering anywhere, by anyone, we should sit down and cry. I am reminded of the callousness that we experience watching the daily news. There is suffering in Rwanda, women are systematically raped in Bosnia, two-thirds of imprisoned men in the United States are African Americans whose children live in poverty. We should cry about these situations, get up and dry our tears and then do our part to challenge the suffering of those less fortunate than ourselves.

Saturday night was the annual *Ta'ziyeh* play. Like the passion play for Christians, this play was an annual event at the school. The play describes the martyrdom of Imam Husayn at Karbala by Yazid's army. Ta'ziyeh is performed only during Muharram and gives the students the opportunity to act out and make real the suffering of the holy family. Through reenacting the suffering, the young people can directly participate in honoring history. Although there was tremendous suffering at the battle of Karbala, Shi'a believe that they were victorious in preserving Islam. They believe that each performance is a commitment to end suffering and oppression and establish justice. The performance itself is considered a revolutionary action and redemptive as well. At the school, boys and girls were allowed to work freely together, presenting the play. Historically in Iran, men and boys played the role of women because it was believed that women shouldn't act publicly.

The students had practiced for a month, some memorizing long monologues. The most sought-after roles were Yazid and Zaynab. The high-school girls had all memorized the arguably feminist speech given by Zaynab, the Prophet Muhammad's granddaughter, after she was captured and numerous children were taken captive at the court of the despised Yazid, who refused to recognize Ali as the caliph. It is believed that it was Yazid who was responsible for the death of Fatima and her unborn child. Later, after a ten-day battle, Yazid was responsible for the murder of Husayn, all his male next-of-kin, and their supporters. They were shot with arrows, cut to bits by the swords of the enemy army, and ultimately decapitated. Their heads were put on spears and paraded through Damascus. Dehydrated survivors, mostly women and children, were taken in chains to Yazid's court, where Zaynab gave her famous speech.

The students gave an amazing performance, eliciting tears from the audience. The audience weeps as a response to the story, encouraging the students and energizing the performance. The students reenacted the fight scene, the wailing women, and the dehydrated little ones.

This play expressed the epic tale of murder, sorrow, and justice, but not everyone agreed with teaching young children about such horrors. One friend of mine was born in Morocco and raised in a Sunni family. After she married her Shi'a husband, she "converted." She expressed a tremendous fondness for the ahl al-bayt but was very disturbed by the practice of chest beating and face slapping. She told me that one day during Muharram she picked her daughter up from school and she was sobbing. Her daughter was extremely upset because Imam Husayn had been murdered. My friend explained to her daughter that Husayn had died a long time ago, trying to put the story into some context for her. She felt that the sorrowful stories, although true and important, were too much for the mind of a young child and caused her daughter to have nightmares.

Another convert, Karen, also felt uncomfortable with any aspect of self-mortification. She stressed that she was able to participate in the sorrow of the ritual but that she could not make herself participate in any hitting or slapping. She believed that this was a cultural practice, not a religious one.

Everyone was in agreement that the Karbala story is an important one to be told and that Muharram is a time to acknowledge the suffering of all people and vow to stand for justice.

The Ashura rituals performed during the months of Muharram and Safar encompass a variety of practices that lament the martyrdom of the ahl al-bayt. These rituals are considered to be pure worship but sometimes communicate a political and religious statement expressing piety and resistance to oppression, an important issue in the community. The rituals provide a symbolic vocabulary, as in more recent protests in which the Shah of Iran was likened to Yazid, the caliph responsible for the murder of Imam Husayn. Today Shi'a practitioners liken Saddam Hussein to Yazid and are not happy with George Bush either. Every person that I interviewed was thankful to be an American because they were allowed to express religious freedom. Under Saddam Hussein, people were persecuted and murdered. Some of those I interviewed had half their family missing or imprisoned. That did not make them agree with President Bush's bombing of Iraq. Many believed it was a poorly thought out plan that made things worse rather than better for most Iraqis because the basic infrastructure of the country was being destroyed. Besides, bombing on the first day of Muharram would be similar to bombing the United States a week before Christmas. This seemed especially inappropriate to them because the rituals of Muharram serve as a reminder that one must always fight against oppression and injustice and mourn those that have been martyred.

These mourning rituals are important because they honor the martyrdom of family members today in Iraq. The mourning rituals allow participants to acknowledge change in the immediate situation and imagine the afterlife. For the Shi'a, rituals that commemorate the ahl al-bayt do not create closure but instead keep the ahl al-bayt alive through their prayers and actions. They maintain a direct relationship with the ahl al-bayt that transcends the temporal world, for they believe that the ahl al-bayt is present at all rituals in their honor.

In particular, this understanding is invaluable to Shiʻa women because it affords them the opportunity to be in direct contact with their spiritual role models. By enacting their rituals they experience a sense of their own spiritual and political agency. They place great importance on the fact that it was Husayn's sister Zaynab, granddaughter of the Prophet, who was the first to hold a majlis, the mourning lamentation still performed today. This allows women an important role in the development of Shiʻa Islam, giving them voice and power. This year, it helped soothe the sorrow they experienced as yet again their holy land was being destroyed.

During the months of Muharram and Safar women hold majlis and invite others from all the various ethnic communities. At these functions the different grieving styles and rituals are mixed, each community adding its own specific style. Elegies in Farsi, Arabic, and Urdu are chanted. American-born women have written elegies in English with perfect rhyme, following the same melodic patterns as those written in other languages. They take turns speaking, chanting, and leading matam (chest beating), but all sit together and weep. Although each group has its own flavor, there appears to be a shared understanding that transcends language and culture; during this time the intention is the same for everyone—and that is the expression of love and sorrow for the ahl al-bayt.

The pain of the azadari ritual is not a pain of punishment; it is a pain of participation and mutuality by which the ritualist joins in the suffering and martyrdom of the ahl al-bayt. This pain affects the individual and the society and, in the case of the Shi'a, establishes a place in the culture and religion that creates religious separation from the Sunnis, thereby transforming their identity. The lament is a reminder of past suffering that is still alive in the body, heart, and mind of every Shi'a person who establishes union with the ahl al-bayt.

Through the weeping and wailing inspired by the azadari, the suffering is made real and is embodied in the female participants. Whether the tears are shed for the symbolic loss of the past or for current sorrows in their lives today, the lamenting process allows women to express the emotion of grief, to shed sympathetic tears that are healing for self as well as the community. It is a means of protesting against oppression and injustice that have existed historically and continue today. The azadari ritual unites the participants through *body prayer* and bonds them physically and spiritually.

Participating in the events of Muharram establishes the women's piety and reaffirms their ability to make sacrifices and to protest all forms of oppression. A Shi'a friend of mine from the community who was born in Iran and educated in Britain insisted that the observation of Muharram was a reminder to "stand for a just cause, however bitter." She found great solace in the Ashura rituals.

The azadari ritual connects the community of women through a timeless ritual that is a response from the heart of the women in the community for suffering and atonement. As a participant I felt that the rituals created a sense of togetherness in which I could "rest in the arms of Allah" and an environment where we could all shed tears without shame. Based on love, the tears that flow during the azadari ritual wash away the sorrow of all women that participate, enabling them to shape culture and history and to position themselves as creators of the next generation. These rituals and role models help them to construct meaning in their lives, creating solidarity across diverse ethnic groups. Although these women do not share the same languages or customs, their shared religion bonds them and transcends cultural differences. Participating in the rituals gave me a new look on grieving and community, which made intimacy possible when people come together for a shared cause.

As I headed toward my car, I felt exhausted yet full of love. I had experienced participating in the Muharram ritual, complete with sorrow, tears, and a profound sense of relief. Perhaps it was the cathartic release of tears that made me feel deeply relaxed and at peace with our universe even though I knew that there were still people all over the world suffering. At least this small group of people were honoring such suffering with their religious rituals. As I fumbled for my car keys I felt a hand on my back. "Sister, I am having a majlis at my house tomorrow after school. Would you like to come?"

"Inshallah. God willing," I responded with a smile.

THE IRANIAN WOMEN

nitially it was difficult for me to tell the difference between the Iranian and Iraqi women. They wore the same clothes—long black abayas, headscarves, and chadors. But as time went by, I learned that there is a tremendous difference. Iraqis are Arabs and Iranians are Persian. Although those countries share borders, the cultures are quite different. What many residents of that area have in common is Shiʻism. While Iraq is approximately sixty percent Shiʻa, Iran boasts ninety-nine percent and has a Shiʻa-led government, hence the name, the Islamic Republic of Iran. Most of the Iranians I met had come to the United States for an education and had stayed or they had followed their husbands here. As a group they were quite educated, and at the school I never met an Iranian that hadn't gone to college. In Los Angeles, jokingly called Irangeles or Tehrangeles, there is a diverse Iranian community, many of whose members are not religious at all. Yet most of the Iranians and Iraqis from the school professed that they had become more religious after moving to the United States.

From 1941-1979 the shah of Iran made every effort to Westernize and secularize his country, to such a degree that women were forbidden to cover. This was especially difficult for older women who had covered their entire lives or for deeply religious women who believed that covering was a mandate prescribed by God. There was a high unemployment rate for educated men whose wives went "public," working in short skirts while the men stayed home. This was humiliating to many Iranians. Religious people vied for control of the government, and in 1978 Ayatollah Khomeini came into power. He encouraged Iranians to take back their culture and religious habits. Unfortunately, like the shah, he rescinded choice from the people and enforced an Islamic Republic. Initially Khomeini rallied support from women who chose to wear the chador as a sign of solidarity, opposing the shah's regime and the imposition of Western influence. Unfortunately, he decreed that veiling was mandatory, thus abolishing freedom of choice for women.

My first encounter with an Iranian family was as a guest of one of the ten-year-old girls in my Arabic class, who invited me to attend a Muharram ritual. Nasrin had spent many days teaching me to wash and pray, and explained to me what was going on and why. She was the first person to ask me to stay after school for my initial majlis and was the first to tell me, "Just try to cry. If you do, our lady Fatima will love you forever. If you ever have problems after that, she will help you." This simple statement was reminiscent of my own childhood love and devotion to the Virgin Mary. As a child I believed that Mary was always with me, guarding and protecting me. I found great solace in her image. My first name was, after all, Mary, just like my other four sisters. My dear mother, unable to get pregnant immediately after marriage, prayed to Mother Mary for fertility. Her prayers were answered with twelve subsequent pregnancies.

I felt somewhat shy as I entered the house of my new Iranian friends. Like many homes I visited in the Iranian community, it had light carpet and light, upholstered furniture. There was little art on the walls, mainly calligraphic verses from the Qur'an and plaques that named the holy family in Farsi or Arabic. Most of the Iranians I met were fluent in Farsi, the language of Persia, now called Iran, as well as in Arabic, the language for prayers. Of course, everyone except the old grandmothers spoke English and many spoke French or Spanish as well. Majlis held in the homes of Iranian and Iraqi women are similar to those held by Pakistanis. The ritual itself does not change, but Iranians and Iraqis do not have small rooms converted into *imambargahs*, or altars, as the Pakistanis do; instead they make their living rooms into sacred space, where their presence and prayers create a holy environment. Iran and Iraq boast numerous holy sites, tombs, and shrines of the ahl al-bayt and the Imams, so immigrants from these countries say that they don't need replicas like the Pakistanis. For those lucky enough to live in Iran or Iraq, they can make *ziyarat* (pilgrimages) whenever they wish.

Some homes have a room that is completely cleared of furniture and the carpets covered with white sheets, and everyone sits on the floor, but others leave their furniture in place, sometimes adding more chairs to receive the maximum number of guests. Chairs are placed against the walls of the room, creating an empty circle so that women can see the *zakireh,* the woman that chants the elegies. Depending on the home, their majlis have a more formal setting. The zakireh is well versed in deeply moving laments that elicit tears in the participants.

Nasrin was thrilled to have me visit her house and meet her family. After I met her father, he quickly disappeared, for this was, as usual, a ladies-only event. At the gathering, the majority of women were from Iran. They arrived completely covered in long black chadors but, upon entering, removed them; many were exquisitely and expensively dressed in black. One woman wore a black St. John knit suit, black stockings, and black high heels, in contrast to the women from the school, who wore plain black abayas. She and her well-dressed friends wore exquisite jewelry covered in diamonds and pearls and looked incredibly elegant. One woman had a two-inch collar covered with jewels around her neck. Their jewelry might be a pendant with "Bismallah" (In the name of God) inscribed, but it would be encrusted with diamonds, rubies, and pearls. This pageantry seemed to indicate that for some Iranian women, majlis are a social affair as much as a religious one. I was told that some of the women that came that day were not very religious and just came to the functions the way some Christians never attend church except on Christmas or Easter.

The more religious women and young girls wore long black dresses, and some had black lace dusters that were very pretty. Even though they were dressed in black they had an angelic quality about them. Little girls wore velvet dresses or miniature abayas. Tiny babies dressed all in black wore hijabs and bands tied around their foreheads with salutations to Imam Husayn written on them. One of the sayyed's babies had a gold amulet with a large diamond pinned to her clothing for protection against jinn or the evil eye. If they were sayyeds, the little boys wore the floor-length white *deshdasha*, complete with a turban and a thin gauze overcoat just as the adult males did. It established them as direct descendants of the Prophet Muhammad.

After the laments and prayers, we dined on *fesenjoon* (chicken in pomegranate and walnut sauce), jeweled rice, kebabs, and a cake with layers of fresh fruit and flavored with rosewater. It was on this day that I would first taste what would become my most favorite candy, *sohan*. There was a tin of sohan brought from Qom in Iran and also a homemade version. Sohan is a saffron-flavored brittle, also called butter fudge, crispy and chewy at the same time.

After I had known Nasrin's mother for over a year, I asked her how she came to live in the United States. She told me her story, and my eyes brimmed with tears. Her family left Iran shortly after the Iranian revolution, moving first to London and then to the United States. She divulged that for years her heart was still in Iran, where her grandmothers had taken her, as a child, to the beautiful shrines for prayers. She said that as time passed she has realized that Islam lives in her heart, and she carries it wherever she moves. She told me that this epiphany was a turning point in her life. She no longer missed Iran; the United States was her home. This was my first experience with an intimacy that I later shared with many women in the community. She explained that her parents had left Iran because of the religiosity of Khomeini's regime. I was surprised to hear a devout Shi'a make a comment like this. She told me that her family was very religious indeed but that Shi'a are quietists and don't belong in politics.

The next day I was invited to a *sofreh*. Sofreh, whose name literally means "tablecloth," is a form of nazr, a vow to do a good act in return for an answered prayer. These functions are hosted any time of the year or specifically during Muharram and Safar, to express thanks for intercession. Most commonly they are in honor of Fatima, Zaynab, Sakineh (Roqayyeh), or al-Abbas. For the women, nazr is a pledge giving thanks for shafa'a, divine intercession, as they seek solutions to their personal problems. Sometimes Hazrat Fatima will appear in a dream, so in her honor a sofreh is held. The women vow to do a good act or to refrain from a bad one. Their prayers are especially valid in sacred space. In the Iranian/Iraqi community a pudding made with rosewater is served when a woman's prayer has been answered. If you receive a bowl of pudding you must make a wish; if that wish is answered the following year, you must vow to serve at least fourteen bowls of pudding, in honor of each one of the Fourteen Infallibles, (the Prophet Muhammad, his daughter Fatima and the twelve Imams who are the direct descendants of the Prophet Muhammad. One year I received a bowl and my friend told me to make a wish. If it came true I would be responsible for making fourteen bowls the next year. The following year my wish did come true: I landed a year-long job taking American students abroad. I went to my friend and told her that my wish had been granted, and I asked her how to make the pudding. She said, "Oh, just make a pudding with some saffron and rosewater, a little cornstarch, and sprinkle ground pistachios on top." "Are you kidding?" I responded, knowing I needed a recipe. She laughed and said, "Just go to Costco and get a big tub of ice cream for everyone. That will be good enough!"

Food is an important cultural element, and prayers are whispered during cooking and before eating. It helps believers remember their good fortune while continuing to feel sorrow for those less fortunate. Sharing food is a means of socialization and bonding for women as they discuss their daily lives, their families, jobs, and joys and frustrations over what it is to be a wife, mother, and woman. Not once did I attend a function where food was not offered. At many big events people will pay to have food catered for hundreds of people because they will be rewarded in heaven for doing so.

One of the more beautiful ceremonies I attended was an *Jashn-e Ibadat,* which marks and celebrates the day that a nine-year-old girl is given her first hijab, or headscarf. Initially the little girl to be honored, Nadia, wanted to wait until she was ten years old to wear hijab, because she was on an ice-skating team. Being on the team meant that she couldn't wear hijab during competitions and shows. However, as soon as she turned nine, she changed her mind. Having two older sisters who wore hijab, she wanted to cover her hair to be like them. Her parents tried to dissuade her. They warned her that she would probably not be allowed to perform on the skating team because she would be out of costume, but she insisted on emulating her older sisters.

At her insistence, her parents allowed her to hijab, and the party was planned. It was a lavish affair with well over one hundred women and girls in attendance. Twenty girls were dressed in floor-length, white gowns with flower wreaths on their heads, ribbons trailing down their backs. They walked down the aisles of the new masjid carrying candles and Qur'ans. One little girl scattered rose petals as she walked toward the altar. The masjid had just been purchased from a church, and the pews were still in place, making the ceremony reminiscent of a Catholic wedding or a First Holy Communion. The girl receiving her first hijab strolled down the aisle like a combination bride and princess at a coronation. As she approached the large chair where the imam usually sits, she turned and smiled at her tearful mother, who had converted twenty years earlier, climbed up onto the chair and seated herself as if on a throne. Poetry was read, her mother gave a speech, and sisters and friends poured blessings upon her in the name of the Prophet Muhammad's daughter Fatima al-Zahra.

After the ceremony was over we all moved to a large hall for a reception. There was a complete meal made by her father and his friends, followed by a cake that looked like it should have been made for a wedding. I sat at a table with women from Iraq and asked them if they had had this sort of ceremony when they were young girls. They laughed and one said, "This is an American thing. Where we are from there is no ceremony." They added that most of them had never worn hijab until they moved to the United States as adults.

This informal conversation showed me the difference between cultures and how Islamic rituals can become Americanized to fit the changing needs of the community. The creation of such a rite-of-passage ritual marks a child's entry into religious responsibility and commitment. It allows her to assume the identity of a woman by donning the hijab and also establishes her as a Muslim. She is now visible as a Muslim, which differentiates her from mainstream religion and culture in America. Adopting the hijab also makes her identifiable to other Muslims. This child was very proud to participate in the ceremony and wear her scarf.

One morning I received a phone call from a friend at the school. "Sister," she asked, "will you come and help with the body of an Iranian woman? She has no daughters to wash her." I knew that a non-Muslim should never wash the body of a Muslim woman. When I expressed my concern that I might not be Muslim enough, she said, "Sister, you are one of us. Haven't you made shahada?" Shahada is the first pillar of Islam, and, yes, I had taken shahada. By saying, "La ilaha illallah" (I bear witness that there is no God but God), I had taken the first step to becoming a Muslim. Of course I had uttered "La ilaha illallah" many times, but I still never felt Muslim enough. She assured me that I was Muslim enough, so I went to a Catholic Funeral home to wash the body of a very old, pale-skinned Iranian woman.

I felt tremendous gratitude that I was asked to participate

in such a sacred rite. The woman we washed was eighty-eight years old. She had left two sons behind when she died. With no daughters or females to wash her body, the sacred task was left to the community of women. Apparently there was a shortage of women available to do the washing, so I was called to help.

The first washing was done for cleanliness; we used a bar of Ivory soap. We washed the entire body with soap and rinsed it off. The next washing was with warm water that had powdered bay leaves mixed into it. Before each washing, we made the niyyat (intention) and then recited some prayers. The washing and rinsing process was done in rounds of three. Water is poured over the right side of the body, front and back, then the left side. The next washing was done again with warm water that had camphor in it. Again we prayed as we rinsed her, three times on each side. The last washing was of clean, pure water, again three times, starting on the right and moving to the left.

She had two sons, no daughters. Was she a grand-mother? When did she come from Iran? She was obviously Shi'a but was she religious? It was humbling to have such an intimate relationship with a woman I had never even had a conversation with. I didn't even know her name, but performing this service made me feel a sweetness toward her. I couldn't help imagining washing my own mother's body, the tears, the regrets, the love, and the closure I might experience.

Two pieces of fabric were wrapped around her legs, and a top piece was brought down like a blouse with a sash tied around her waist. A piece of fabric was cut into a triangle to make her a headscarf. We rubbed her forehead, knees, and feet with the powdered bay leaves and then camphor. We then wrapped her in one large piece of cotton, which we tied at both ends. There was a very old Qur'an open on the counter. We stood in front of the Qur'an and asked for forgiveness for her sins and then asked that we be forgiven if we had done something to her body that was unintentionally inappropriate. Working mostly in silence with whispered explanations, I experienced the living relationship between the women and their religious beliefs.

I thought about my own mother's death. Would I be allowed to wash her or would she end up in some anti-septic environment, touched and prepared by strangers. I could feel tears welling up in my eyes. I had never really thought about my own mother's death. Now I thought to myself, this is a wonderful way for achieving closure. I imagined that I could weep as I washed her body and how intimate and real it would be. How I could lament the times I had been unkind and critical of her. I fan-tasized saying good-bye to her and how much I would miss her. All her small faults that irritated me seemed so silly and trivial. I sat down, crossed my legs, and cradled my head between my arms and started to cry. My friend came to me and touched the top of my head. "Is it too much for you, Sister?" "No," I replied with a slight smile, "I am just thinking of my own mother and how much I love her. I hope that someday I will have this honor with her." After we wrapped the woman in muslin fabric and put the scarf around her head, we all went home to shower before attending the funeral.

I drove past archangels and giant flower arrangements as I entered the cemetery. As I drove around the corner my Muslim friends couldn't be missed. The Iranians were dressed in long black chadors that billowed in the wind. I could see that some of them were crying. The Muslim cemetery had no angels or statues, no poetry or flower arrangements. There were just plain markers on the ground. There were specific prayers and a procession. I was escorted to the grave, dragging my black chador in the dirt, trying to keep from stumbling. I watched as the men carried the woman a few feet and set her on the ground. This was repeated three times. "Why do they do that?" I whispered. My friend said, "Oh Sister, we do not want her to feel that we are rushing her to the grave, so we stop and let her rest for a moment." The dead woman we placed in the ground, in no casket, by her sons. From dust to dust, I assumed. Her head was set on a pillow mounded from dirt, facing Mecca. Prayers were offered and tears were wept. My favorite prayer was uttered: "*Inna Lillahi wa inna ilaihi raji'un*" (We belong to God and to him we shall return).

Typically, women are not allowed to be close to the grave. However, as an outsider, I was allowed to stand at the edge and have every detail explained to me. One of the women who invited me to the funeral pushed through the crowd of women about thirty feet away from the grave, dragging me behind her. She explained to the presiding imam that I was doing research on the Shi'a community, and it was important that I get a clear view and correct information about the ritual. I was dressed in a long black abaya, and when he looked at me, he wrinkled his nose and shrugged his shoulders and said, "Why not?" During the funeral I felt a sadness that I was not really a part of this intimate community. Once again, I had participated in their world, partaking in a beautiful and sacred ritual. Afterward, I found myself hanging around waiting, but I did not know for what. Perhaps it was a longing to be a part of the community as an insider. It meant a great deal to me to be invited to participate in their world.

Most of the American converts I met were married to Iranians. Their husbands had come to the United States to attend college and had decided to stay. These women had a different perspective of the rituals and were not as active in the Muharram rituals as the immigrants were. They attended but rarely beat their chests or displayed excessive emotion. "I love the holy family," one woman told me, "but I can't relate to the hitting oneself and face slapping. It's not my culture, but I go anyway to express my love and commitment to the holy family." I became good friends with this woman. She was a wonderful mother, full of energy, and loved her husband dearly. She had fallen in love with him when she was only seventeen, and after she married him it took her nearly twenty years to convert. She told me that she had been raised Southern Baptist but liked Islam because it seemed to have all the answers.

As winter approached I was invited to my friend Fatim's house. Born and raised in Iran, she had come to the United States for college and fallen in love with a colleague who was also Iranian. They married and she stayed, even after divorcing him, in the United States.

She was one of the few divorced women that I knew at the school. Fatim was extremely bright and had a master's degree and Ph.D. She taught at a Southern California university. Her three lovely children lived with her. Late in November she invited me to her house for Thanksgiving dinner. We had an incredible feast and then we all sat down to watch a movie. While the kids decided which movie to watch, she and I looked at her wedding photos. I was shocked to see that, in the photos, she was not wearing hijab.

She explained that when she was young, during the seventies, she was not religious. "I came from a secular family. It is after I had children that I started to change my mind about religion. I like being part of the community," she explained. "It's mostly the human relationship. I guess it's, I don't know, cultural. Because we are so individualistic here [in the United States], we don't even know our neighbors. We think that it would take away from us if we help others, but it doesn't. What goes around comes around, and we don't realize it here. 'I don't care about downtown Los Angeles, those poor people down there.' It's not like that. Everybody is connected; we all care about each other. In Farsi, the Iranian language, there is no such word as 'I don't care'; we don't have this expression at all. You cannot translate it. The closest thing you could come to is 'It's not important.' But you just don't have 'I don't care'; it does not exist in the culture at all—it doesn't exist in the language. We don't have that. I feel a tremendous love in our community and it makes me feel safe and happy."

We settled down to watch a movie that was so sad, we all sat and cried. It felt good to me to be able to cry with her. One of the things that I really liked about the Shi'a community was that they cried without shame. They were not afraid to show emotions; it was culturally acceptable for men and women to weep. We got up and had more food, then decided to watch another movie. It was nearly one in the morning when I got up to drive home. The entire family hugged and kissed me, then the youngest said, "Will you come for Christmas?" I was surprised to hear that they celebrated Christmas. "We don't really, but we put up lights every year." Their mother looked at them and said, "Well, if Sister Bridget wants to come, we can even put up a tree. After all, we are all Americans." Clearly, like many people, she did not see Christmas as particularly religious but as an American celebration. My Arabic teacher told me that, when she was growing up in Lebanon, her Muslim family put up a Christmas tree and had parties for their Christian friends every year. "They would fast with us some days and then we would all eat together at the end of the day. Our neighborhood was mixed [Christians and Muslims] and we didn't have problems like we do today," she said with a grimace.

THE IRAQI WOMEN

Much of my learning about Shi'ism came from my having, early on, befriended the principal of the school. She was an Iraqi Kurd. I knew nothing about Iraq or Kurds and very little about Shi'ism. This woman graciously invited me to study Arabic at the school, visit her home, and meet her extended family. She was no-nonsense and rock solid in her beliefs and demeanor. She was serious yet loving, and even though I was fifty years old I felt as though she saw me as Julie Andrews in the role of Maria in the film *The Sound of Music*. She would shake her head at my never-ending cultural faux pas yet continued to invite me to participate in her world. I believe that she could recognize my sincerity and the deep curiosity I held about her religion.

Married to a surgeon whom I only met once, she had five children, and they lived in a mansion. The kids ranged in age from junior high through college. The swimming pool was empty and used as a skateboarding ramp where her children, girls and boys, skated endlessly. At school she never wore anything but black, so when I was invited to her house and she had on a beautifully patterned, long velvet dress, I was surprised. I was even more surprised by her long, elbow-length hair. We sat in her living room and she served me tea and something made from phyllo dough stuffed with meat, maybe the Iraqi version of a samosa.

Although these Iraqi Shi'a are considered extremely religious, Liyakat Takim, in his book *Shi'ism in America*[1], says that they are very open-minded and allow women many opportunities to participate publicly, whether that is in the workplace or at the mosque. Evidence of this was the principal's daughter Safa's behavior. Safa had a mind of her own and was involved in sports. Among other things, she skateboarded and snowboarded, even making a film about Muslim snowboarders. She was a free thinker with a great sense of humor and would end up graduating from UCLA with a degree in architecture. Although Safa's mother was very religious, she was also very realistic, encouraging her daughter to remain pious and to express herself as fully as possible. She saw her as the future of Shi'ism and the future of the world, contributing to Iraqi and American culture.

The Iraqis were a tight-knit group. The young women joined the older women as they interpreted their religion in a way that would encourage modernity yet allow tradition. It was not unusual to see the Iraqi women lead gatherings, organize Quran study groups, and speak at mixed-gender religious events. Shi'a women know their religion and are actively involved in the perpetuation of it. The most common response to one of my dissertation

---

1. Liyakat Takim, *Shi'ism in America* (New York: New York University Press, 2009).

questions, "What are the benefits and the detriments of living in the United States?" was a unanimous agreement that the most important benefit was religious freedom. For many of the Iraqis this was the first time they felt free to be openly Shiʻa, cover their hair, and hold religious gatherings publicly. Saddam Hussein had made their lives miserable, imprisoning entire families or organizing the disappearance of family members.

The Qazwini family was one such family. These Iraqi Shiʻa from Karbala were religious leaders and a threat to Saddam's regime. Numerous members of their family had been imprisoned or disappeared. I had the good fortune to meet the brothers and their wives and was often invited to their homes for gatherings. Years later, when I needed to build trust in other Shiʻa communities, I could name drop the name of the Qazwini family and would receive instant acceptance. On one occasion I was invited to one of Sayyed Mustafa al-Qazwini's house for a women-only gathering.

When I arrived at the house, I was surprised to see a modest home in a lower-middle-class neighborhood. There were dozens of cars parked everywhere. I entered the house and, after removing my shoes, was greeted by dozens of women. The living room was completely emptied of furniture. Sheets were tightly spread across the floor and women sat against the walls. After a fairly short gathering reciting the laments, shedding tears, and offering salutations, we sat down to eat. As at all the dinners we had, people sat on the floor, where lengths of plastic were laid out. The plastic was like a tablecloth the length of the room and about three feet wide. We sat on both sides, facing each other as we ate. When we finished, the plastic was rolled up and put in the trash.

As usual, the food was delicious. The feast included Iraqi-style kebabs, numerous salads, rice, and beef, lamb, and chicken entrees prepared in thick, spiced sauces. There was an enormous platter three feet in diameter, covered with fresh fruit and nuts. Dessert was rosewater-flavored pudding and multiple types of baklava. The hostess told me that much had been cooked the day before but that she had been up since four in the morning. "We say prayers over the food" she said. Her friend giggled and added, "These are superstitions, but they really do work. When we cook, we ask Allah to answer our prayers and then of course we pray in thanks, when our prayers have been answered."

I excused myself and wandered into the kitchen, always curious to pick up some culinary skills from Middle Eastern women. A young woman approached me and asked if I was the teacher writing the book. I said yes and she grabbed my arm. The woman told me that she had been a hairdresser in Iraq for years. When she moved to the United States no one would hire her because she covered her hair. "In Iraq, we have ladies-only shops, but here in the United States, men and women are in the same room working together. In Iraq, when I was at work I didn't need to cover my hair at the salon because it was ladies only. Can you help me?" she begged. "Can you go on Oprah and tell my story?" I explained that I didn't have connections to the popular Oprah Winfrey television show, but this was a familiar conversation. The Shi'a women often told me that they felt misunderstood by everyone, including other Muslims. They were happy to have a non-Muslim represent them. "After all," one woman told me, "everyone will listen to you because you are an American and a teacher, with very white skin."

It was baffling to many women that I wasn't married. The Prophet said that marriage was part of his *sunnah*, the tradition. It is seen as a responsibility of every man and woman to get married and produce children. Wasn't I lonely, they asked. When I said that I was widowed once and divorced once, that was acceptable. A number of women chuckled and said that if their husbands died, they wouldn't remarry either. This seems to be a fairly common response from women all over the world when I tell them why I am single. At least I had children who, in turn, would have children someday. That was the most important thing, to be a mother and a grandmother.

The next day at school there was an incident I will never forget; I'm sure the other women won't either. Even though many of the rituals inspired tears, there was always time for laughter. This time, I came to school for the afternoon gathering ready to cry my eyes out. I was completely dressed in black, wearing my chador that I was so fond of. When the women saw me, one of them started to giggle and said something in Arabic. Everyone looked at me and burst into uproarious laughter. I was completely bewildered. "What is it?" I asked. My friend explained to me that my chador was inside out and that the label could be seen. "What is so hilarious about that?" I wondered. "Well, that is how you wear it if you are a prostitute or looking for *mut'a*, a temporary marriage." Again peals of laughter, and one woman said, "Stay away from my husband. No, actually you can have him!" More laughter ensued and off I went to the bathroom to turn my chador around the right way.

When I got into the prayer hall they were still giggling and had clearly told a number of other women. I received the typical kisses on each cheek and some big hugs. I was happy to know that my friends had such humor whenever I did something that was culturally inappropriate. I asked Sister Zahra why they thought it was so funny. She explained the custom of mut'a to me. Without a husband, I might be interested. Of course they knew I wasn't but still thought it was funny. Zahra explained that historically the Prophet Muhammad suggested temporary marriages if necessary, especially when one travels. One traveling man, that is. Married men can initiate it but married women can't. Technically in Islam sex cannot take place outside of marriage. Zahra explained to me that mut'a is rarely done anymore, especially in the United States. I asked her what she would do if her husband wanted to have mut'a with someone else. Her response was immediate. "Oh, I would divorce him and take him to the cleaners," she laughed. "I'm an American citizen!" I became so fascinated with the concept of mut'a that I used it as a research question for my dissertation. Of the thirty-six respondents, only one said that she would allow it.

Actually, it made sense to me that, assuming you believe that it is a sin to have sex outside of marriage, you would want to have a temporary marriage sanctified by shariah law. Temporary marriage is problematic when a young girl commits to it. In cultures where virginity is extremely important she will have a difficult chance ever marrying. It can also be a form of prostitution, but from my perspective it made sense, because after one experiences mut'a the woman must be celibate for three months. A contract and dowry are executed, so if the woman becomes pregnant the man is responsible for her and for the maintenance of the child. For an older woman, it could be a great pleasure, the joy of having sex without a permanent marriage and the housekeeping that comes with it.

I felt that polygamy had its place as well. It made sense to me that there was an appropriate time in history for multiple wives. The Qur'an states that a man can take up to four wives as long as they are treated equally and justly. Today few Muslims continue this practice, especially in the United States, since it is illegal. Most rules have historical significance, and during the Prophet's lifetime, when women couldn't care for themselves, it was the appropriate thing to do. When there is a shortage of men it would also be appropriate. This being said, I never met an American Muslim woman that would tolerate it.

While at the school, I was diagnosed with skin cancer on my face. Unfortunately, I was treated with Efudex, a cream that eats away the cancer and generates new cells. I had an allergic reaction to it, and my entire face became an oozing, pussy sore. If I cried, my skin burned; if I talked or smiled, it was excruciating. I couldn't get any sun on my face or even florescent light, for that matter. It felt like I had a hot iron against my face, it burned so much. When I went to the university I was attending, no one said a thing. It was as if I looked the very same. When I went to a gathering that afternoon at the Shi'a school, women came to me and hugged me. "What happened?" they asked, some with tears in their eyes. "Will you be ok?" I explained that I was receiving a treatment for skin cancer and had a serious reaction to the medication.

"Come with us; we will pray to the holy family to heal you." We entered the hall and there were already dozens of women there. They circled me while others came to see what was going on. They started to chant, some started to cry. I too had tears flowing down my cheeks, which increased the burning and created more pain. I was so moved that they cared about me so much. A woman came rushing forward into the group, speaking in Arabic. The other women let her pass through. She had a large purse full of baby wipes, diapers, a cell phone, and other miscellaneous items. Finally she pulled out a small vial of a soft, pale brown, powdery substance. She opened it and poured some into her palm. "Sister Bridget," she said, "this is sacred soil from Karbala. . . . Don't worry, it is pure; there is no pee-pee in it." She started to very gently rub it onto my sores. I was profoundly grateful to receive such love and care from the women and, at the same time, cringing inside. I was sure that my dermatologist would disapprove of such healing interventions. The women hugged me and kissed me. "Don't worry, Allah will be with you. Don't be sad; be brave, like Zaynab!" Over and over I was reassured that I would be healed because, like them, I loved the holy family. I had proven myself by my commitment to learn about Islam and participate in the

Muharram rituals. Besides they had petitioned Fatima to intercede on my behalf.

A year later I attended a gathering at an Iraqi woman's house. I arrived late and everyone was sitting in a circle, drinking tea. My friend took my hand and paraded me around the room, jabbering in Arabic. Of course I didn't understand much of what she was saying, except "ahl al- bayt," "Fatima," "Imam Husayn," and "Ya Allah!" The women smiled and said, "Masallah!" They all smiled and nodded their heads. I asked my friend what she had said to them. She said, "I am telling them to look how pretty you are, your face so beautiful, with sparkling skin and a lovely smile." I felt a bit embarrassed and tried to pull away, muttering, "Thank you, thank you." After all, what could I say? She pulled my arm again, dragging me through the room, again speaking in Arabic. This time the women gasped, some yelled out in Arabic, and a few burst into tears. "What?" I exclaimed. "I told them that just one year ago you had cancer all over your face and that you have been healed by Allah and the holy family!" she said. Women jumped out of their chairs, hugging and kissing me. Some lifted their cupped hands in prayer. "Ya Allah," they prayed. "Ya Allah." I burst into tears and felt incredibly cared for. "Come, sit here," said the hostess. "You are our guest of honor today."

Not all events elicited tears. One year I was invited to a Mother's Day swim party at the home of a very wealthy doctor. His wife, although educated, was a stay-at-home mother with three lovely young daughters. She invited me to attend the swim party at her house. The house was a typical Southern California mansion equipped with hired Mexican help and a gigantic pool. I marveled at the young mothers flying down the slide with young children in their arms. It was like any other all-American scene except that the fence around the house was much taller than in most American yards and afforded modesty for the women and girls. Of course there wasn't a man in sight, and as usual the food was incredible. Halal hamburgers made with Middle Eastern spices, cake, ice cream, and watermelon, along with ten other side dishes. It was fun for me to see another side of these families. I had initially met them in the prayer halls, where we had wept and lamented, performing the commemoration rituals for the holy family. Now we were cavorting and splashing in a pool on a hot summer day. The old grandmothers, like many grandmothers everywhere else in the world, sat fully dressed, fanning themselves and holding youngsters wrapped in damp towels, caressing their hair and gossiping in Arabic.

While at the university I had to undergo scrutiny from the Internal Review Board. The IRB, as it is called, is an institution developed for researchers, to insure that they are ethical in the field. There are numerous rules and regulations that must be adhered to in order to protect the people interviewed or used for experiments (as in the case of medical drug trials). I needed to have each woman that I interviewed sign a release form. Most of the women couldn't read English well enough to understand the jargon, so they were very hesitant to sign anything. Iraqi women, especially refugees, had been interrogated by Saddam Hussein, then by the Saudi government, and finally questioned as they entered the United States. The last thing they wanted to do was sign something I presented. I had to plead with the IRB for special permission to interview them without a release form. Ultimately, it was decided that if I interviewed the women and taped the conversation, I could ask them in the first recording for permission, promising that their names would not be used. As the community began to trust me, they said they wanted their names used. They wanted their stories told!

The IRB also insisted that I interview the women in a public place like a library or restaurant. This was not an issue for young American-born women or those that had grown up in the United States, but the older women felt uncomfortable. For those from cultures where women are homebound, it was difficult to understand that I wanted to meet them in a restaurant. Why wouldn't I go to their homes? Ultimately, I realized that this was insulting to them. Who in their right mind would go to a restaurant to eat when they could stay home and have fresh food they had made especially in my honor? Food is one of the best perks of researching women from the Middle East. It is also the source of a great sense of pride, and a gift of love to those who eat it. Ultimately, after many arguments with the IRB, after persuading them that, culturally, women were insulted if I refused to go to their homes, I was allowed to visit them for interviews. The opportunity to visit someone's home gives tremendous insight into who they are, their level of education, and their economic status. But the most important aspect of home interviews is that they allow for increased intimacy. I looked forward to every invitation and often met three generations of women living in the same house.

One day I was invited to a woman's house for tea and sweets. By American standards it was a five-course meal. The door was opened by one of the woman's sons and he asked me if I was looking for Umm Hassan. I said no, I was looking for Safiya. He laughed and said, "That is Umm Hassan." When she appeared I was very confused. Umm, she explained, is the name given to a woman when she becomes a mother. Safiya was the mother of Hassan, hence, Umm Hassan. I was invited to the living room, where there was very little furniture, and we all sat on the floor. Next to me was a very large, older woman who had a face so wrinkled that she looked like an apple doll. Under her chin were tattooed dots. I had seen these tattoos on the older women's faces on other occasions and remembered that the Prophet Muhammad had said that tattoos are haram. If so, why did women tattoo? My friends had explained to me that these cultural markings were overlooked by many people, and women kept with their traditions. At this point, I knew better than to question an old woman. I bent over and kissed her scrunched-up face. "Asaalamu alaykum, Umm Safiya," I said. She gave me a look of dismay that continued for quite some time. Her daughter laughed and said that she was not Umm Safiya but Umm Ali, her mother-in-law. "We are called Mother of our first son, not our daughter," she told me. "We call our fathers by Abu, father of Ali, the first son." It seemed that at every occasion I learned something new.

As we sat down for tea the old woman eyed me with

suspicion. Was I married? Did I work? Where were my children? Was I a grandmother? As she received the answers from her daughter, she just grunted and scowled. After half an hour of politeness I asked if I could start the interview. The entire conversation between Safiya and me was in English. Periodically, her mother would interrupt in Arabic, apparently demanding a translation. Finally, the grandmother became increasingly irritated. I asked Safiya if she was angry with me and apologized for not speaking Arabic. Safiya laughed and said that her mother thought that I was there to interview her! After all, she was the matriarch of the house. I apologized profusely and asked Safiya to translate for me.

"May I ask your age, if it is not too rude?" "How many children do you have?" "How many grandchildren do you have?" "How long have you been in the United States?" She answered laboriously and became agitated. Her voice became louder and she started asking Safiya questions, gesturing wildly with her hands. Safiya looked at me and gave a chagrined sigh, "She wants to know, why are you asking so many questions? She just wants to tell her story." I apologized again and she started as Safiya translated.

Umm Ali told me that she hated Saddam Hussein. She hated George Bush too. Saddam had come to her village and rounded up everyone and taken them to a remote area in trucks. The men and women were separated into different areas and they were all put in a circle. Saddam's cronies went around asking, "Who is collaborating against Saddam?" When no one answered they went up to a woman and shot her. They asked the question again.

This time Umm Ali said that people started pointing at total strangers just to save their own lives. She told me that if you lived, you would suffer forever if you falsely accused someone to save your own life, but people were terrified and didn't know what to do. Needless to say, tears poured down my cheeks. She told me that she walked with one of her daughters and two grandchildren to a town where they were hidden until they could escape. Later, they spent years in Saudi Arabia, in settlement camps, until they moved to the United States. Umm Ali told me that if your mother was literate you could learn to read and write. If she was not, you went uneducated, coming to the United States with no way to make a living. The story was depressing at best. She looked at me and wagged her finger: "Now, you go tell *that* story in your book. Let people know how we have suffered because we are Shi'a!"

The next year I was invited to a gathering at an Iraqi home where many Iranian women were present. They were dressed formally and well coiffed. Most of them wore heavy makeup and did not cover their hair. The hostess told me that they were not very religious but had purposely attended the gathering to petition Lady Fatima. There was the usual sequence of events, with nowehs read and tears cried. At no time did any of the women perform matam. As the afternoon drew on, the hostess asked me if I would perform matam so that the Iranian women could see what it was. I said, "No, matam is not a performance, and I feel uncomfortable being on such display." She left and returned a few minutes later with a tear-streaked face. "Please," she implored, "my friend's daughter has been in a coma for two years. Please pray to Lady Fatima to help her." I told the other women, and a few of us made a circle and began the ritual. Soon women were slapping their chests, and tears were plentiful. We petitioned Lady Fatima to restore the young girl and to release her mother from such suffering.

It was these kinds of events that held the community together. One Iraqi woman, Taibeh, had grown up in Iran because of persecution of Shi'a in Iraq. She became a close friend to me and taught me a lot about Shi'ism and the role women play in maintaining the religion. She was often asked to lead the gatherings. Her sermons were in Arabic, Farsi, and English, and she could chant nowehs in Arabic and Farsi. We all sat down for a round of tears if she was the leader. On one occasion she had the entire room crying. Following her lament, three Pakistani women chanted a noweh, followed by more tears and sobs. They finished by turning toward Mecca with the usual *salawat* (prayers). The Iranians and Iraqis participated in their part and the Pakistanis in theirs. At the end, everyone tried to respectfully follow everyone else, but women continued to cry. Compared to the other majlis I attended, I had never seen such uncontrollable weeping. I must have had a quizzical look on my face, because my friend leaned toward me and whispered, "This majlis is in honor of Bina's sister, who died last year." I, too, began to cry harder when I realized that we were petitioning Bibi Fatima to deliver the sister's soul to heaven. Although Bina was Pakistani, she worked at the Muslim school, where many of the children were Iranian and Iraqi, hence she knew both communities of women. No matter which community the women were from, in this mixed group there was one intention that the women shared, all participating for one same reason: they adored the ahl al-bayt and turned to them as intercessors and role models, which helped them to comprehend their own sorrows.

Taibeh explained to me the importance of her commitment to Islam. She said that she had wanted to attend college and be a therapist, but she married, had kids, and never got around to it. She believed that as a spiritual leader in the community she could help alleviate suffering, and she did. From her perspective, azadari was therapeutic. I agreed: Where else can a group of women sit and weep collectively with no shame? The collective expression of sorrow, whether historical or personal, is healing. She told me, "Normally that is the case when you are crying—you are crying for a couple of reasons. Crying is not a bad thing. Whenever you feel depressed, if you cry a little bit and try to get over it, it's, you know, cleansing, psychologically and spiritually. It is also about love even in the face of oppression. If you let your soul free and you let your third eye be opened, you see Islam is something that touches your heart. It is the love that Imam Husayn expressed for Islam that makes him great. He, himself, is like the morning prayer."

It was the Iraqi women that first taught me the rituals and laments. I would forever be fond of their style of commemorating the holy family. Like the martyrs of Karbala, many of the Iraqi refugees had suffered horribly for extended periods of time, yet they had balanced sorrow and loss with hope and faith. They were able to weep and wail, yet joke and laugh moments later. Their love of their religion allowed them security in an unsure world.

THE PAKISTANI / INDIAN WOMEN

Fatima invited me to attend a majlis at her aunt's house. I arrived at what appeared to be a typical Southern California tract home, upper-middle class. The grounds looked like those of every other house in the neighborhood. The yard was well groomed and there were flowerbeds bulging with pansies, snapdragons, and poinsettias. Under the shade tree in the front yard was a bench with a statue of a small girl holding a basket. As I walked up the sidewalk to the door I saw a banner with "Welcome" emblazoned on it. The house looked like every other all-American home on the block. When the door opened I was greeted with hugs and kisses from my hostess. This is new to Pakistanis; they do not usually kiss on both cheeks like Middle Easterners, but it is becoming more and more a part of their culturally blended tradition. The living room was completely decorated in whites, off-whites, and pastels and looked like the room of a Disney princess. I took my shoes off, as is the custom, and stepped on the plush white carpet. There were large bouquets of pastel flowers on tables and pillows with gold, pink, and blue embroidery. I was the first person there, and she invited me come in and have tea. Early on, when I started to attend the gatherings, I would arrive promptly at the stated time. I learned, as time passed, that arriving an hour late was probably wiser. It seemed that everyone else arrived late by American standards.

I was happy to see that Fatima's niece Masooma was there. A college student, she stood there in well-fitted jeans and a t-shirt, her head covered with a massive amount of curls. I had never seen her hair uncovered before and delighted in its beauty. At the part of those thick black curls was a stripe of neon blue, the latest Los Angeles hair fashion. It always surprised me how hip and cool these college women were. Seeing them covered in black at the mosque or prayer halls had left me with stereotypes that later embarrassed me.

She jokingly told me that she was studying engineering, her only other "cultural" choices being accounting or medicine. I laughed when she said this, understanding the joke that children of immigrants were often pushed into these fields of study. She said that school was going great and that she especially loved her Spanish class, telling me that she wished she could become fluent. I told her that she should go abroad for a semester. "Are you kidding?" she exclaimed. "My parents would never allow that. That is why I live with my aunt during the week. I go back to my parents' house on the weekends." I had heard this before; most parents did not want their daughters to live alone in apartments.

When I interviewed the immigrant mothers, their single main concern was for their daughters' safety. Although they claimed that they loved the religious freedom that they were afforded in the United States and the wonderful quality of life, they worried endlessly about sex, drugs, and, as their daughters jokingly added, rock and roll! Most girls lived at home until marriage, but some of the more liberal families let sisters and cousins get apartments together. It was rare that anyone went out of state for an education.

Masooma offered me a glass of mango juice and we sat on the couch and talked about her life. She said that her parents had had an offer of marriage for her but she had refused. She wanted to finish college first, get a job, and then get married. "After being married for a few years I would like to have kids," she told me, "but probably only two. I really want a career. I know what you're thinking," she laughed. "How American of me!" Interestingly, very few of the young women wanted to get married young; they wanted to finish school, first and foremost. We sat and talked for half an hour before the next guests arrived, and then we were ushered into a small room that was perhaps a den or an extra bedroom.

In many homes Pakistani and Indian women have special rooms that have been emptied, where they have created an imambargah, an altar, specifically for Muharram gatherings. The rest of the year these rooms may be used solely for prayer but more typically revert back to a spare bedroom, office, or sewing room. They are especially dedicated spaces for ritual observance. Those who live in Iran or Iraq can make ziyarat (pilgrimages) whenever they wish, but for the Pakistanis, their ziyarat must be done symbolically through the imambargahs. These replicas are symbols that create a visual relationship with the holy family. I asked Fatima where she got all the beautiful objects to decorate the room and she told me that they were specially made in Pakistan or India.

The room in Fatima's house was especially beautiful, a miniature version of what was found at the centers. Somehow Fatima's husband had managed to drill holes in the paneling so that tiny lights appeared around the altar. When the rituals were finished for the year, they could close louvered doors, hiding everything until the next year. The shallow closet-turned-altar was incredibly beautiful, and they allowed me to photograph it. We stayed there for about three hours. There were only about twenty-five women in attendance. There were no children present, and the environment, even though the women lamented and cried, was quite peaceful. There was an obvious softness in the atmosphere, quite different from the intense matams that I had been to at Pakistani prayer halls.

Fatima took my hand and led me to the room where the rituals would be held. The walls of Fatima's room were hung with carpets, tapestries, and paintings of prayers written in Urdu, Farsi, or Arabic, calling for the commemoration and blessings of the martyrs. White sheets were spread over a carpeted floor, covering the entire room. They were pulled tight and smooth. A small carpet was placed in front of the altar, so that the zakirehs (reciters) would have a place to sit or stand. There was a chair draped in black cloth for the special zakireh to sit on and recite her tearful lament. The wall that was especially created for the ritual was covered in black velvet. Hanging on the walls were black and dark green velvet banners that had the names of the holy family embroidered with gold thread.

On the back wall of the imambargah were *alams,* standards representing the holy family. The best of these alams are sterling silver hands with the palm facing front, covered with the names of the ahl al-bayt written in Arabic or Urdu. The number of alams differs but the goal is to have one alam for each one of the Fourteen Infallibles—Muhammad, Fatima, Ali, Hasan, Husayn, and the other Imams, leaders of the faith who were direct descendants of the Prophet Muhammad.. There are also alams for members of Husayn's party who died, such as al-Abbas, who was killed trying to fetch water for the dehydrated children. The alams had fabric draped from them like flags and were adorned with flowers or prayer beads. Some alams were small enough to fit into a box or large enough to use for a procession. Tiny cradles for the baby Ali Asghar, who was murdered in the arms of his father Husayn, were set in the imambargah. Fatima told me that the objects would remain in place for the first ten days of Muharram and then would be carefully packed away until the next year.

That night we drove into Los Angeles for a majlis. The prayer halls were quite large, with separate sides for men and women and an additional room where food could be prepared and served. In the Pakistani and Indian centers, called *Zaynabias* or *Husaynias*, after Zaynab and Imam Husayn, an imamabargah is similar to a shallow, narrow stage, covered by a curtain that can be drawn across it when rituals and prayers are not being practiced. The walls are hung with embroidered tapestries and there are large, ornate alams. The alams are much larger than the ones in homes, and in some imambargahs there are large replicas of tombs and shrines of the Imams. During Muharram there is a coffin draped with a white cloth spattered with red paint to represent the blood shed by Imam Husayn and his family. The women take great care in the building and maintenance of these altars. If the center has separate sections for men and women, they will each have their own imambargahs. The women, however, maintain both sides.

The Pakistani and Indian women wore plain black shalwar kameez and no makeup or nail polish. Occasionally there was someone with a lacey top or a small pattern on black, but typically it is seen as more pious and respectful to wear a perfectly plain black cotton shalwar kameez (or Punjabi, as they are called in India) with a long *dupatta*, the shawl that also works as hijab. Generally these women were more relaxed about covering their hair than were their Iraqi and Iranian friends, and their scarves fell to their shoulders even in public. One woman explained to me that when one is sad and depressed one doesn't feel like getting up, putting on makeup, or doing one's hair. Not doing these things proves that you are truly sorrowful and grieving for the holy family.

The only jewelry I saw was sometimes a ring or pendant around the neck made from a special stone that holds protective powers. The necklaces are engraved in Arabic with the names of the ahl al-bayt: Muhammad, Ali, Fatima, Hasan, and Husayn. These stones, called *aqiq*, are from the Middle East and they protect the body from mental and physical harm. They bring good health and good luck, and, according to the women, the Prophet said that if you wear one of these stones when you pray, Allah will hear your prayers. They are brought to the United States as gifts, and women from all the different ethnic groups wear them. As the years passed I received many *aqiq* stones engraved with the names of the holy family and parts of the Qur'an as gifts. To this day I wear an *aqiq* ring with "Allah" engraved on it.

My friends explained to me that during the first ten days of Muharram each day is devoted to a different member of the holy family or one of the members of Husayn's party who died in the battle. In front of the imambargah there was a small carpet where the zakireh sat. Three women offered a noweh, or chant, in honor of Bibi Fatima, as the Pakistanis call her. Next, three other women chanted in soft, childlike voices, representing Sakineh, Imam Husayn's small daughter. In the story of Karbala, Sakineh pleads for water, for her life, and for her family. Sakineh relates the tragedy of Karbala, which includes her sorrow for the murder of her infant brother, Ali Asghar. This story reminds the listeners of their moral and ethical responsibility to fight against oppression. The lady of the house or her daughters play an important role in facilitating the oral history of the community. Often all the female members of the family will spend months practicing nowehs that are recited in Urdu. The modern generation has translated them into English and some have created their own.

Women are considered especially successful if they can elicit strong emotions and tears among the *azadars* (mourners) when they recite. Through narrative a response is elicited among the participants, which gives women in the community a strong and important role. The majority of nowehs are through the holy women's experiences, especially those of Sakineh and Zaynab, who survived the massacre. As the story was told, women called out a salawat asking for blessings upon the Prophet's family; this was the next lament chanted, from the perspective of Hazrat Zaynab, the sister of Imam Husayn. The cantor reenacted the suffering of the thirsty martyrs as women wept, moved by the sorrow of the narrative. It was easy to cry, the stories were so sad.

On this evening there was a procession through the room, with young girls carrying the alams and a small coffin draped with a white cloth spattered with red paint to represent the blood of the martyrs. Next, a silver cradle was carried through the room, commemorating the baby Ali Asghar. Women touched and kissed these symbols with great respect. When the majlis was over, the women moved to imambargahs and touched the alams and miniature shrines, offering prayers and money. I was particularly moved by these gestures. I could not help imagining the women all over the world who had wept over their losses of family, property, and safety.

Removing the scarves from their heads, the women stood up and started to beat their chests, crying out, "Husayn, Husayn" in a call and response. The chest beating became more aggressive and the weeping stronger. Some of the women hit their chests so hard that they became bright red. Younger women moved their dupattas to the side so that they could slap their bare skin.

As one group tired, another group moved forward. The more intensely the nowehs were chanted, the stronger the response from the participants. They encouraged each other by calling out "Hai, Hai." I had never seen such violent chest beating in any group. It was almost a machismo response by the younger women. I was later told by my friend Fatima that this is frowned upon and that it is an interpretation of a new generation. "We always beat our chests," she said, "but never violently."

The crying became wailing, and women stood and sobbed. All at once everyone seemed to know that the matam had ended, and there was a quiet peace in the room. Each woman turned and pointed her right index finger toward Mecca, uttering a prayer. These final prayers are again ziyarat, the pilgrimage of the heart, blessing Fatima and her family. They are named one by one.

This was in sharp contrast to a wedding that I attended after Muharram was over. There are no celebrations during Muharram; they are postponed until the respect has been given to the Prophet's family. It would be considered very disrespectful to celebrate during this time of sorrow and grieving, so festive events are held during other months.

The night before the wedding we held a henna party. Everyone had their hands hennaed; the bride's were especially elaborate. We sat and visited, laughing and talking, as the bride's mouth was stuffed with sweets. At the wedding the women had the most beautiful clothes I had ever seen. Their *saris* and shalwar kameez were covered in sequins, pearls, rhinestones, and other jewels.

Some of them were entirely embroidered and covered in handmade braids and trims. The fabrics, mostly silks, were of every hue and color imaginable.

The women wore gold jewelry studded with diamonds, rubies, and emeralds. Many had dozens of gold bangle bracelets on each arm. Those, too, were often covered in jewels. Many of the women had baubles hanging from their ears that resembled tiny bells with jewels dangling from them, so that when the women shook their heads or laughed, the jewels moved in a delightful manner. The women had long black hair braided with chains and pearls and sometimes flowers. At the end of the braid was a jeweled tassel. For those women that were older or wanted a more elegant look, their hair was in a large bun at the nape of the neck. Again, jeweled ornaments decorated the buns. The bride wore the most exquisite dress, made of gold and turquoise silk. It was covered with jewels and embroidery. She wore a scarf tightly framing her face and then another veil draped over her head. The veil was edged with diamond-shaped points, completely jeweled, framing her face. She was the most beautiful bride I have ever seen, dressed so differently from the typical American bride dressed in white.

However, there was something disturbing about the bride; she kept her eyes cast down, looking miserable. As she was paraded through the room with her small bouquet of roses in her hands, she was met with oohs and aahs, but I felt increasingly concerned. Earlier in the week she had begged me to attend the wedding. She had been so excited and happy that it seemed really odd that now, at her own wedding, she looked really unhappy.

It took me about twenty minutes to get next to her. I discreetly whispered in her ear, "Are you okay? Are you sure you want to go through with this?" She turned her downcast head toward me and smiled, saying, "I'm supposed to be sad; I'm showing that I am sad to leave the home of my parents . . . it's our culture. Trust me," she whispered, "I'm faking it," as she flashed a huge grin then looked back down at her bouquet.

Earlier that year I met two other girls at the Pakistani masjid who were engaged to be married. Both of them were in their first year of college. We sat outside the masjid on a warm summer night, the scent of jasmine surrounding us. They smiled shyly as they told me that they had performed nikkah. "We are betrothed Islamically," one said, "but haven't had our traditional weddings yet." The other explained that in Islam many people do not date before they are married. Marriages are arranged. She told me to imagine it in the same light as if they were engaged. "We don't date but are promised to our spouse," she said. They both said that they were waiting for their husbands to finish college. That way they could support their families. "How long must you wait?" I asked. "At least two years," one exclaimed, "but we are already designing our dresses and choosing gold jewelry."

The Pakistani and Indian communities are very close-knit. Although they participate with Iranians and Iraqis, they have their own distinct traditions. Their concept of ziyarat is different from that of women from the Middle East because, unless they have the financial means, they have not had the opportunity to travel to Iran and Iraq and visit the shrines of the Imams. In the Pakistani community women hold majlis all day, traveling from house to house, finishing at the center in the evening. The gatherings are open to everyone. When I said that I had not been formally invited, I was told, "You are not invited to church, but you go—it is the same here, we cannot turn anyone away." On a given day the first majlis started at noon and ended with lunch, but other women had started as early as 9:00 a.m. The remaining ones began at 2:00, 4:30, and 7:00 p.m.; then everyone went straight to the center. Many people left one gathering at 9:30 so that they could drive to another center, where the majlis lasted until midnight. These gatherings last for the first ten days of Muharram and then are sporadically held over the next two months until all the martyrs have been commemorated. I tried to go to as many as possible, but it was exhausting and I was gaining weight at a rapid pace. My love of Pakistani and Middle Eastern food got the best of me. And crying so much, so many times each day, was tiring in itself. However, bonding with women and sharing stories made it magical for me.

One Saturday I was invited to attend a majlis in the early afternoon. I drove into an obviously wealthy neighborhood. When I approached the house there were already dozens of Mercedes and Lexus automobiles lining the street. I entered a house that was beautifully decorated, and I was introduced to about six female medical doctors who appeared to be related. When I asked the hostess if she was a doctor she laughed and said, "No, that would be my husband and the rest of my family." Her hands held a platter of samosas, and she asked me to follow her downstairs. The lower level of the house was a gigantic game room. All the furniture had been moved out, leaving a pool table at one end and a large, wall-mounted TV screen at the other. There were already many women and children gathered. We sat on the floor in a semicircle, facing the imambargah. What I was about to witness came as a great surprise to me.

The ritual started in the usual fashion, but this time three sisters between the ages of seven and ten stood in front of the women. They wore identical black outfits. As they started to chant I felt as though I had been transported into a heavenly realm. Their voices were angelic and the chanting brought tears to my eyes. As they finished and sat down, another four girls about the same age got up and repeated the performance. Again, they were angelic. Of course there was no applause because, after all, we were supposed to be sad and grieving.

I asked the woman next to me who the girls were. She explained that they were cousins and that they had spent the year memorizing the recitations. It was a spiritual status symbol to have one's daughters emulate the rituals, keeping the tradition alive from generation to generation. When they were finished, the girls sat and ate with us. After the feast was finished, they went upstairs, where I later found them playing with Barbie dolls. It was amazing to see how rapidly they moved from sacred space to the ordinary. I had seen this in all the communities: when the ritual was finished they returned to the ordinary world, doing ordinary things.

That day I was offered a delicious drink. I asked the hostess what it was and she explained to me that each day a special food is prepared in honor of the martyrs.

On the day that commemorates al-Abbas, the cousin of Imam Husayn, who was killed as he begged for water for the children, a delicious drink called sherbet is served. A mixture of milk, ground pistachios, almonds, and *rooh afza* (rose syrup) quenches the thirst after matam and weeping. This special drink is served in memory of the babies that suffered without milk when their mothers were murdered or taken to prison. Soon I was able to recognize staples at every occasion, such as nuts and fresh dried fruits, as part of the offering.

My friend Nina asked me if I wanted to go the Husaynia with her and I gladly accepted. She gave me directions; we were to meet at 9:00 p.m., when the activities started. There were over one hundred cars in the parking lot and it was nearly impossible to find a parking place. Finally, as I entered, I saw an immaculately clean entrance not unlike a church lobby. Women had a separate entrance into their own room, where the male speaker is televised. As with the Iranian and Iraqi women, their rituals are private and unobservable to the male gaze. Whether at home or in the center, the women form a semicircle facing the imambargah. They removed their scarves and their lamenting process was extremely physical, something that, if witnessed by men, would be an intrusion to their sense of privacy and sacred space.

On this particular night I sat next to a young Indian girl, Umbreen. She had arrived late because she had participated in a concert at her high school. Umbreen had an exquisite voice and was the only Muslim in her school choir. I told her that I thought that women were not supposed to sing publicly and she shrugged this off.

"Our religion is an internal process," she said. I watched Umbreen get up and beat her chest very violently that night. I asked her why, and she told me that she was beating the sins out of herself. In all the time I had participated in the Shiʻa community, I had never heard such an explanation for matam. She explained that it was the same idea that Christians have when they emulate the suffering of Jesus when he died on the cross. "Sure," she said, "you have seen these Christians enacting the suffering of Jesus. Well, I do the same." Umbreen was one of the young women who carried the mock coffin on the last day of Muharram. This was a tremendous honor for her, and as she set it down she knelt, touched her head to the black fabric, and wept.

I imagine that participating in the ritual helps Umbreen make sense of human suffering. She performs the self-mortification of chest beating as penance for the sins that she may have committed against others. Without really saying so, Umbreen is asking for redemption through her participation. On the way home I asked my friend Nina if beating one's chest and weeping would wash away one's sins. She told me that it would not and that the azadari ritual was never meant for this but that this is how some people interpret it. From the perspective of a teenager, Umbreen's participation in the ritual must have a sincere meaning. She creates this meaning by participating physically. The ritual ties her to the Shiʻa community even though the rest of her life is lived in a fairly secular fashion. Her participation allows her a spiritual identity in a profane world.

After we finished at this center, someone suggested

that we go to a place called Bab al-Ilm. Bab al-Ilm translates as "The Door [or Gate] of Knowledge." It was nearly midnight but I couldn't resist. These Pakistanis had rented a small building in an ordinary neighborhood that appeared, by the Spanish signs on the buildings and stores, to be primarily Mexican. As we entered, women were sent through a curtain to their own side. I could hear the men lamenting, beating their chests, and chanting in unison. The women seemed to be extremely intense in their chest beating and some had actually pulled their shirts open, baring their chests. They slapped their skin with the palms of their hands, leaving red marks and, in some cases, breaking blood vessels. The women seemed to be in competition to show who could be the most pious. I was relieved that my friend's son was driving us the one-hour ride home. It was 3:00 a.m. when I crawled into bed.

This was the kind of day that I would experience while attending Muharram rituals in India. The Indians and Pakistanis share many similarities in their cultural interpretation of the ritual practices and sacred space and symbols. They execute chest beating very intensely, like the men that I saw in centers and parades in Los Angeles. I heard that, in both countries, men cut themselves, although the women did not, nor did I witness this in the United States.

I was hired by Long Island University to teach Islam for one semester. While we were in India I had the opportunity to attend the Muharram rituals; the most amazing was on Ashura. Ashura, known as Martyr's Day in India, is a national holiday. I invited my students to accompany me, but only one agreed to do so. We started off that night in a rickshaw accompanied by a young Muslim guy that we had met at the neighborhood market. He assured us that he would take good care of us while we were there; how, I wasn't sure, because he would not be allowed to enter the women's side. Muharram in Delhi would include the intense, bloody type of rituals that I had read about but never seen in California.

The first night, we were taken to a neighborhood where there were three separated buildings: a Hosaynia, a Zaynabia, and a Fatimia. We went from site to site, pushing through thousands of people. Each building was beautiful in its own way, but the one dedicated to Fatima was my favorite; I considered it the most splendid. Almost every room in the hall was covered with mirrors, and garlands of flowers were draped everywhere, giving off a heavenly scent. There was a magnificent chandelier in the room; it was bright yet emanated a soft glow. There were no carpets on the floors, just smooth, clean marble. The atmosphere was soothing, but what struck me most was an incredible breeze that blew gently even though there were no fans on and no windows. The air outside was dead still. It reminded me of the readings I had done of saints describing the smell of roses and a soft breeze although no saint was present—at least no divine being visible.

On the eve of Ashura we traveled to a famous Shi'a center called Punja Sharif. The building is three stories high, with an open roof. The opening allowed fresh air to circulate, and from the top two floors, observers could look down at the participants. There were mostly women on the second floor, and on the third floor was a mixed group of men, women, and families. There were also cooks on the third floor, all men, stirring enormous vats of rice, meat, and lentils. On the ground floor the rituals took place. In one corner were thousands of candles burning. The thick scent of incense and huge bouquets of fresh flowers permeated the air. One side of the room was lined with smoked-glass mirrors. About three inches away from the mirrors hung long garlands of fresh flowers. Even though there were hundreds of people in the room, the scent was heavenly. In a separate room was a white horse with layers of flowers around his neck. The horse was drenched with red paint, symbolizing the blood spilled by the martyrs.

When the ritual started the white marble floor was spotless. Families led little boys, probably ages three to five years, into the center of the room. The boys' shirts were removed and the boys were each given a small wooden handle that had chains attached to it. At the end of the chains were tiny blades shaped like fat crescents. The children each held up one arm in the air and took the blades and hit themselves around the back. The parents and other relatives showered them with praise and affection. The boys smiled and were picked up and paraded around the room. At no time were they hurt or in danger. They were praised for the early emulation of what was to come.

As the crowd grew larger the intensity became epic. Young men strutted onto the floor, taking their shirts off and tucking them into their pants as they began to beat their chests. They then used the same instruments the small boys had used, but larger, and because they had the strength that the children did not have, they drew blood. They whipped themselves into a frenzy. When it appeared that someone would pass out, a team stopped the individual and took the cutting instrument away. They washed his wounds, gave him water, and sent him to rest. Hundreds, if not thousands, of men repeated this throughout the night. Periodically the blood was washed off the floor with a hose, the floor was dried with a giant squeegee, and the process would start again.

In shocking contrast, the women stood above and watched. They talked on their cell phones, gently beat their chests, or visited with friends as their children wandered around freely, seemingly unaffected by what was happening below. As I was talking to my student, a woman asked where I was from. When I told her that I was an American she said, "Oh, I'm from England. We come home every year for Muharram." While we stood and visited, two young girls came by, pointing below, laughing. She started to laugh, too, and when I asked her what they were talking about, she pointed to a young man below who was shredding his bare back with blades, very rhythmically with a thrust chest, almost like a choreographed dance move. She said, "They think he is really cute and are wondering if he is looking for a wife!"

As midnight approached, the streets filled with tens of thousands of people. They carried elaborately decorated coffins and banners, representing the martyrs. A horse was led through the crowd and many people carried immense alams. It was much more magnificent than anything I had seen in Los Angeles. It was now 1:00 a.m. and we were exhausted. As it was too late to find a ride home, we slept on the hard floor. After we had slept for about two hours, the chanting of salutations to the martyred holy family started again. The women around us stood up and started to beat their chests and weep. Finally, at 5:00 a.m. we went into the streets and walked to the train station and back to the youth hostel where we were staying. I posted a note on my door:

Dear Students,

    I will not accompany you to the university for classes today. I need a day off!

Ya Husayn!

A year later I would return to California to participate in the Ashura rituals again. I was invited to a *jalous*, a procession, through the streets of downtown Los Angeles. This procession was during the day and started in front of the county courthouse. Compared to processions in India, it was highly organized; there were police guarding the participants in the same way they did for any parading or protesting group. It was a mixed group of Shi'a, all wearing black. They too carried banners and replicas of coffins and even stopped to pray. They had obtained a parade permit from the city of Los Angeles, and the streets were theirs for a few hours as they, too, in a less extravagant manner than Shi'a in India, walked through the streets shouting, "Ya Husayn!"

    When I discussed the contrasts between processions in India and those in Los Angeles with the American women, they all agreed that things were different in the United States. I was told, "As American Muslims we do things differently." Every immigrant group brings traditions and then Americanizes them. One woman said, "In a way, they are cultural habits mixed with the religion. For example, in India, we used to cook food for the poor during Ramadan and Muharram, but there are no poor among us here in America, or at least we cannot see who among us is poor."

Much of the Muharram ritual process and azadari are ethnicity-based. Converts that are American-born do not typically participate in them as fully as the foreign-born Shi'a. Language is a barrier, and matam, the beating of one's chest and slapping of one's face, is a cultural practice more than an Islamic one. In my observations, some converts would beat their chests gently, but I never saw one become as engaged as those who had been born and raised Shi'a. However, Louise, the German mother of a large family we met in Los Angeles, was quite articulate about the evolving experience she has had since she converted over twenty years ago. She fully participated in all the rituals.

Married to a Pakistani man for over twenty years, Louise was recently told that her cancer, that had been in remission for some time, had reappeared. She told me that her faith had helped her immensely through her health crisis and explained that participating in the ritual every year with the Pakistani community helped her personally but also gave her a larger worldview of human suffering. For Louise, practicing Shi'ism, especially this time of the year, helped her to be more compassionate but also more of an activist. I spent the afternoon at her house, where we drank tea and ate sweets. She lived in a very modest house and did not appear to have much money, in sharp contrast to most of the other Pakistanis I visited. She explained to me that during the rituals she cried not only for the past but also for the future, because "nobody's learned and suffering still goes on, so I cry for both." She said, "Can you imagine trying to feed your starving child and you can't because you're afraid to be shot? What's the difference between then and now? You would think that human beings would live and learn from past mistakes, but they keep repeating them."

Her children wandered in and out all afternoon, showing her much fondness and giving me tremendous respect. I believe that they were afraid that their mother did not have much time to live, so they expressed love for her in each moment possible. She told me that they took turns driving her to the center for the gatherings but that many days, she was just too tired to go. For Louise, being Shi'a held an important commitment to social activism. Louise had her own radio talk show and considered herself an adamant feminist. She had also written a book about internment camps in Pakistan. She explained that as long as people are oppressed we must fight for the end of oppression and for a just world. After all, that is what the Prophet and Imam Ali had requested of us.

It is sometimes hard to remember how I met a certain person. Over the five years I was in Los Angeles, I probably met two hundred women, and about fifty of them, I interviewed. Some of these women became my close friends. One dear friend was Habiba. Habiba was born in Pakistan and has one daughter and a son. Their family invited me to dinner weekly and took me to many functions in the Shi'a Pakistani and Indian community. Her son, who was in college, was our private chauffeur to these events when her husband was unavailable. The family lived in a suburb of Los Angeles in an all-American neighborhood. She worked with developmentally delayed high school students and sewed Pakistani clothing and wedding dresses for extra money. During the years that I knew her she saved ten thousand dollars to go on hajj, the once-in-a-lifetime trip to Mecca, the fifth pillar of Islam as suggested by the Prophet Muhammad. Just one month before her departure, she found out that the tour company had gone bankrupt, cheating her out of her trip. Naturally, she was devastated. Through her tears she said, "I hope that Allah recognizes the efforts I have made and rewards me for them."

Much of the devotion of pious Shi'a is the merit attained on Judgment Day. They work in this world to be rewarded in the next. I reminded her that Allah sees our intentions more than anything else and retold her the story that she knew well about the seventy-yard scroll Fatima holds at the gates of paradise. "Remember, Habiba," I told her, "Fatima has all your good deeds recorded on that scroll, and on the day of Resurrection, she will stand at the gate, and on the forehead of every human being will be written "Believer" or "Unbeliever." But if you have loved Fatima, "Lover" will be stamped between your eyes, and Fatima will intercede on your behalf so that you are not sent to burn in hell." Unable to respond, she wiped her eyes on the edge of her scarf and said, "You want some Pakistani food, some samosas?" With tears in our eyes we hugged and walked into the kitchen. She said, "I have an Iranian friend who is holding a majlis tomorrow. Shall we go?"

EPILOGUE

n June 2011, I had the opportunity to go for ziyarat with a group of Shiʻa. We were to visit Iran, Iraq, and Syria for a spiritual pilgrimage. Finally, I could visit the holy sites that the women in California had told me about throughout the years. I called my friends in California to make sure that the group I was traveling with was legitimate and they assured me that they were. I was so excited to realize a dream that I had held for so many years. We would visit the holiest cities outside Mecca, including Karbala, second-most important to Mecca for Shiʻa. I longed to see the shrines, tombs, and masjids for myself and also to enter countries typically forbidden to Americans. Ultimately, because there was unrest in the area, we were not able to visit Syria or Iraq, so decided to travel to Iran only.

On the journey were six women and seven men. We ranged in age from fifteen to seventy years old. Each person in the group had his or her own personal reason for visiting these holy sites. To my surprise they were not Iranians, with whom I had always imagined that I would go to visit their homelands, but American Pakistanis and Indians. With the exception of the American-born teenagers, the group was quite religious. Some of them had been to Iran and Iraq before, but for most of us it was our first time. We all met in New York at the airport.

The young people, born in the United States, were very Americanized. One family consisted of a mother, son, and daughter, as well as their grandmother. The mother, only forty-two years old, had been diagnosed with a brain tumor. One year after her surgery, her then twelve-year-old son had Moyamoya, a rare cerebrovascular disease and suffered a small stroke. Her mother, college-aged daughter, and now sixteen-year-old son accompanied her on the trip; they all gave thanks to Allah and the Imamate for saving their lives. Theirs was a journey of faith and gratitude shared by three generations. The college student, who was to become my roommate, wore jeans and a t-shirt. Her brother was dressed just as casually. Their mother wore slacks and a shirt, and their grandmother wore the classic shalwar kameez native to Pakistan and India. I was immediately struck by the beauty of the three generations. The mother and son had both had brain surgery within a year of each other and were going to Iran to give thanks for their lives. It was deeply moving to hear their stories.

I was thrilled to have a college girl as my roommate, and we shared many of the joys and frustrations of being in an extremely religious country. During the three weeks together, we became quite close. She was incredibly pretty, with long dark hair and light brown skin. She could easily have been a fashion model. Both of her parents were Pakistani, and her mother had been raised in the United States. Like most Muslim American college students she felt a spiritual connection to Shi'ism but less of a cultural one. I watched her transform from an American woman with jeans and t-shirt to a fully covered "religious" one during our trip. We agreed that Islam was an interior practice that suggests a certain behavior involving love and compassion. By the end of our journey we both felt a spiritual peace but were honestly sick and tired of having to cover from head to toe in yards of black fabric. Neither one of us believed that we needed to be so bundled up as proof of our piety.

Our tour leader, whom most everyone called Mrs. Maulana, meaning "Mrs. Teacher," was completely covered in a long blue jilbab and a headscarf. She had the face of a cherub and the personality of one too. She demonstrated an endless amount of knowledge regarding Shi'ism.

In our group were college students, an engineer, and a Montessori school teacher from India who had been widowed only a year before. The single thing that they were all most capable of was kindness. They had easily spotted me at the airport because I was the only "white" person, as they often called me. Numerous times they would laugh and say they can't believe a white was with them.

This was the first time I had ever been with Shi'a who did not beat their chests and weep. The only tears shed were those of gratitude and humility. The participants desired to emulate the Imams by remembering acts of kindness and charity. As a group, they were the most generous people I have ever met. No beggar was passed by (there were very few in Iran) without receiving a generous donation. Waiters and hotel personnel, bus drivers and porters were given large tips.

From the beginning of the trip I was surprised to see how relaxed Iranians were. On the flight from Moscow the travelers were predominantly Iranian, and the spirits were high. There were only a handful of women wearing scarves as we boarded the plane to leave Moscow for Tehran, but when we landed in Tehran we all grabbed our headscarves and covered our hair. I was amazed to see a woman openly breast-feeding on the plane. I found this refreshing yet confusing, because most of the Muslims that I have been in contact with are quite modest. Although the Prophet Muhammad encouraged breast-feeding for at least two years after a child is born, I had never seen it done publicly by any Muslim woman.

As we landed in Tehran I put on my long black chador. It was important to me to be taken seriously and to respect the culture and religion. In Iran it is the law that women dress modestly and cover their hair, and initially I gladly veiled. Women in Tehran and at the airport wore a variety of styles, from blue jeans and a fitted above-the-knee jacket with a lose scarf to a floor-length black coat. Many young women pushed the dress code limits by wearing sexy clothes and big bouffant hairstyles with scarves barely covering their hair. They wore lots of makeup and were gorgeous. I remembered reading that in Iran, nose jobs are the number one surgery for women, so I started examining women's faces, trying to guess if they had had plastic surgery or not. Women wore absolutely heavenly perfume, so when you walked through a crowd, you got whiffs of delightful fragrances as if you were walking through an imaginary perfumed garden. These young women were as lovely as the stereotypical image of Scheherazade with their big black eyes and button noses. At the airport I was surprised to see that very few women wore the chador. Although the women wore above-the-knee, long-sleeved shirts and pants, the clothes were quite fitted and very attractive. Not everyone in Iran was super religious like those portrayed in United States media. I was seeing a completely different image in Tehran, a city as modern as New York. Later, in Qom and Mashad, the cities home to the holiest sites, I would see a very different picture.

Families met each other with hugs and kisses and huge, beautiful bouquets of flowers wrapped in curled paper collars. Iranian people are extremely diverse, just like American citizens. It is unfair to assume that they are all religious fanatics that support their government without question. There are many Iranians that are fed up with the political/religious regime currently running their country. Unfortunately, because I was travelling with religious people to holy sites, I did not meet many of them.

The Imam Khomeini Airport in Tehran looked just like any other large international airport. Because we were Americans, we stood in a special line for our document checks. Everyone except me was given permission to leave the airport. I was told that because I am an American citizen I must be fingerprinted. They asked me my profession and I said that I was a teacher of Islam. Three men looked at me curiously when I stated that I had come to Iran for ziyarat. One of them asked me to follow him. I looked over my shoulder and gave a wave to my friends, who looked nervous. They later told me that they were very worried about me. The guard and I walked halfway through the airport, to an office where I was supposed to be fingerprinted. He asked me to wait outside the door, and when he returned he said that, out of respect for me, because I was a woman and a teacher of Islam, they would not touch me for the fingerprints. He walked me back to my group, smiled, and said, "Enjoy Iran." For many conservative Shi'a, it is reprehensible for men to touch women they are not related to. I felt safe and appreciative that my entrance into Iran was first a curiosity and ended as a politeness.

After we left the airport we headed by bus to Qom. We were all tired from our long plane ride from New York to Moscow (where we had a very long layover) and finally to Tehran. But our exhaustion did not hinder our excitement, and by now we had had plenty of time to get to know one another. I was already forming friendships that I knew would last a lifetime. The ninety-two-mile trip was full of laughter, conversation, and snacks brought from an Indian grocer in the United States.

As we entered Qom I was awestruck. The city of Qom hosts the tomb of Fatima Masooma, the sister of Imam Reza. It is a large city, where over one million people live. Millions of pilgrims visit Qom every year, so it is bustling, full of hotels and restaurants. Much to my surprise, Qom had numerous universities for men and women, including theology and medical schools. It was very different in Qom than at the airport in Tehran. There were no tight jeans covered with knee-length jackets or Dior scarves loosely attached. I didn't see women wearing makeup, bouffant hairstyles, or designer sunglasses. Women dressed completely in black and were always covered with big black chadors. Wearing a chador is like wearing a gigantic tent, and I had worn one many times in the United States at Shi'a gatherings, but I had never worn it all day, every day, and it took some getting used to. This was quite frustrating to some of the women in our group, because it was extremely hot and the men could wear just pants and a cotton shirt. As Americans and as Pakistani Americans, these women do not dress with a chador. It is a cultural-style dress for women rather than an Islamic one. The dress code was unfair and un-Islamic, from my perspective.

Qom is the center of the Shi'a *ulama,* the elite group of Muslim scholars, the most popular place for the study of in-depth Shi'a studies, where scholars come from around the world to study. It is currently the largest center for Shi'a scholarship in the world. There are an estimated fifty thousand seminarians in the city coming from seventy countries. Qom has seminaries for women and some non-Shia students. Most of the seminaries teach their students modern social sciences and Western thought as well as traditional religious studies.

As we arrived in Qom we saw hundreds of pup tents pitched on the sidewalks and in parking lots. These tents are the temporary homes of the pilgrims. Every year more than three million visit this holy city to pay homage to the sacred sites. People stay in hotels that range from one to five stars or camp in the roads. I couldn't count the number of families that were sitting on cloths having a picnic. Older people napped while children played, and women served tea that had been heated on a Bunsen burner, all the while laughing and joking. This was in sharp contrast to the tears that I had seen at most of the rituals that lamented the deaths of the martyrs.

When we arrived at the hotel I was so excited to be there that I began smiling at everyone and saying, "Asalaamu alaykum." The men in the hotel were formal with me; after a few days I asked someone to explain that in my culture it is a politeness for men and women to great each other and would be considered rude not to do so. Once we had a mutual understanding, people became very friendly toward me. I'm sure that there was a bit of fascination that I was an American woman traveling with a dozen Pakistani pilgrims.

The first morning in Qom I went downstairs for breakfast and was met by a man who was part of our group. At the time I did not know that he was the man responsible for organizing the trip and was a well-known mullah. He asked me what I wanted for breakfast and I insisted that I would help myself. He insisted that I was a guest and got me a plate full of food. This graciousness was consistent among all the men on our tour. They didn't infantilize us as women who couldn't care for ourselves; their graciousness felt truly sincere. They put tremendous importance on *adab*, the good manners that are critical to Islam. As I walked to refill my plate, an old man spoke to me in Farsi. Of course I had no idea what he was saying. The waiter jumped in and explained that I was an American in Iran for ziyarat. This seemed to baffle the old man, and the waiter repeated the explanation two more times. The old man looked at me with a sideways smile and said, "American people very good." I heard this repeatedly in Iran.

Because we were in an Islamic Republic we could eat anything, as all the food was halal. *Halal* is a concept similar to *kosher* in Judaism. Muslims slaughter their animals using a sanitary, quick death at which prayers are offered and gratitude is given for the loss of the life of the animal that sustains humans. Because all the food was halal, our dietary choices were easy, and the food was delicious. The fruit was most amazing, and as we walked down the streets we could smell ripened melons at every step. Every morning the bakers make and sell their breads as men and women wait patiently in separate lines. The five-minute wait was well worth the time to eat warm bread with butter and sour cherry or carrot jam. One night we spent hours in the mosque and didn't return to our hotel until midnight. The restaurant there had dinner waiting for us. I got my fill of kebabs with saffron rice and roasted tomatoes. It was nearly 2:00 a.m. when we got into bed; just a few more hours until the call to prayer and we would be up again, praying!

Our first jog was to the tomb of Fatima Masooma, daughter of the seventh Imam and sister of Imam Reza, the eighth Imam. The building is covered in exquisite mosaics and has a magnificent golden dome and multiple minarets. The inside is completely lined with geometrically shaped mirrors no bigger than a silver dollar. The carpets are specially made, and one can lie on the floor and look up at honeycombed tilework. A huge mosque has been added to the shrine; the entire area is approximately twenty-five thousand square meters. One could walk for days, and I did, seeing endless beauty.

When we visited Fatima's tomb, women threw scarves onto the top of it. Like the other tombs, it is covered with solid mirrors. Again, there was stillness in the chaos, a way of moving and being moved that was otherworldly. Bodies pushed together and we moved as one immense unit, sharing the same   collective breath, hopes, and dreams, even if they differed from those of each individual woman. I could only imagine why someone was crying—the loss of a child, the death of a husband, and in my case gratitude for being able to visit such a sacred site. There were hundreds of women present, and it was easy to get separated from my friends. Even though every woman wore a black chador, I was soon able to recognize a friend by the kind of lace that covered her forehead. To my surprise there were families sitting together on the carpeted areas. Although there were separated areas for men and women to pray, in the rest of the space, genders were mixed. Even though the mosque was full of thousands of people, there was always a light breeze inside as fans turned overhead. Rosewater was sprinkled on people while incense burned. The space was spotlessly clean and people spoke in whispers. I moved away from my group, feeling claustrophobic as women pushed each other to touch Fatima's tomb. I sat quietly in an area that was sparsely populated and felt an incredible peace. There I was, sitting in silence, when I realized an hour had passed.

In one tomb that we visited I was told that forty sisters had died and been buried there. Our tour leader called this the Tomb of the Forty Sisters. Women carried bottles of perfume with roller tops and drew names on the fabric covering the tomb. The smell was heavenly. This modest shrine was one of my favorites. Although it was small, it was still beautifully decorated with mirrors and looked and felt "antiqued" compared to the magnificence of the larger tombs we had visited. One of the women in our group took perfume out of her purse and began to write something on the cloth that covered the tomb, then began to cry. Her weeping grew stronger and more intense. I could only imagine that she cried for the loss of her husband, who had died just a year before, leaving her with three children. I felt a tremendous amount of love for her though I had known her for only a week.

One night we were wandering through the famous Qom Bazaar when I was separated from my group. The agreement was that if we lost each other we would meet back at the hotel at 2:00 a.m. After looking for my friends for twenty minutes I decided to return to the hotel. I walked down the well-lit streets toward the hotel. Swathed in my long black chador I felt completely safe. Had I been dressed in "Western" clothes, I would probably have received stares and would have been considered very rude for not following the local dress code, but still safe. Being a "white" American pilgrim put me more at an advantage than not. I received nothing but kindness, graciousness and respect.

As I turned a corner I found a sohan shop. My favorite candy in the world! I had eaten this before, when I visited the Iranian students' homes in Southern California. They would bring it back to me when they visited Iran. They told me that someday I would go to Iran and could buy it myself; now, that someday had come!

I stood in an open window for twenty minutes and watched as some men made the candy. It was made from butter, sugar, and saffron; they stirred it in large vats, then separated it into small balls, which the men hand pressed with a large weight until they became round and the size of a small salad plate. The men then dipped the plates into crushed pistachios. One of the men came to the window and, without speaking, handed me a broken piece of candy. Returning to his work, he asked me a question. I am assuming that he asked me if I wanted to buy a tin of candy. I said "I don't speak Farsi. American, I am American. Amreeki, Amreeki." There were three other men working and they all looked surprised. One said something in Farsi, and they all smiled at me and started to chuckle. The man returned to me with a tin of sohan. I opened my purse and tried to pay for it but he refused to take my money. He kept speaking in Farsi and gesturing to take it. All the men smiled and gestured with their hands. I walked through the street, back to my hotel, eating this most delicious treat. I chuckled to my-self, remembering all the people in the United States that had asked me if I was afraid to go to Iran. Interestingly, I felt completely safe walking late at night. Before I left Iran I bought thirteen tins. I gave three away, ate three while I was there, and finished the rest when I got back to the United States. I never gained an ounce of weight, resulting in my belief that the candy is truly heavenly food!

After breakfast we wandered off to the masjid for our first prayers. Everywhere we went I was introduced as a very good Muslim and was asked to pray for people. Of course I cringed when I was introduced this way, thinking that my Sufi studies were nothing like the Islam practiced by these devout Shi'a pilgrims.

One afternoon we visited a women's *houza*, Jamat al-Zahra, a women-only college. Shi'a have always taken pride in the education of women, and more women than men graduate from college in Iran. At the school, young girls wandered around in short summer dresses, shorts, and t-shirts. The high walls of the school kept them secure and guarded them from the stares of men. Here they had complete freedom to study in an environment that was very academic and extremely beautiful. Rose gardens and fountains added to the beauty of the architecture. There were swimming pools and a gigantic gym where women could work out between their rigorous studies. We met a girl from Japan who told us that as a Shi'a Muslim she loved Iran because she could be herself and freely practice her religion in a supportive community. She told us that she wanted to stay in Iran forever.

We stayed within walking distance of the Jamjaran Mosque, which is undoubtedly one of the most incredibly beautiful places I have ever been in my life. The beauty is nearly impossible to describe, and although there are thousands of people there at any time, the atmosphere is calm and quiet. It is large enough to house ten thousand people, with walls almost entirely covered with geometrically cut mirrors, none bigger than a silver dollar and most no bigger than a fifty-cent piece.

After a few days in Qom we took the train to Mashad, the home of Imam Reza's tomb, which is visited by twenty million pilgrims every year. Our seventeen-hour train ride was full of storytelling and laughter. I was able to bunk with the three generations of women that I was so fond of. Being with the three of them was like staying with the famous triple goddess in pagan times. Each one of them represented an aspect of femininity that was specific to her age. The grandmother was not only physically gorgeous but full of joy, patience, and wisdom. Whenever there was a problem she would smile, shrug her shoulders, and exclaim, "Let's see it as an adventure!" Her granddaughter, a sophomore in college, was as American as apple pie, so would sit and gently grumble about things that were not like "back home." Jokingly, we wished we could just get a cappuccino somewhere, and her brother kept asking, "Why aren't there any Burger Kings in Iran?" Everyone kept a sense of humor as we lurched along the tracks.

The most frustrating thing about traveling by train was that all the stops were scheduled to coincide with prayer times. Everyone tumbled out of the train after repeated knocks on the door to wake up. We had to pull our chadors over us and walk into the station, where we were to perform ablutions and then pray. The bathrooms were filled with dozens of women using the toilets and then washing. There was water all over the floor and, as at any other train station in the world, the smell was not the best. Navigating yards of black fabric on a wet, slippery floor was no easy chore. Everyone prayed and then we were back on the train, complaining.

Without a doubt, Mashad, also known as the City of Paradise, is the most beautiful home of tombs that I have ever seen. Imam Reza's shrine seems endless; one could easily walk throughout for days. People sleep on the carpets and the atmosphere is highly organized by volunteers. I was told that there are twenty thousand people on the volunteer waiting list. It is believed that by serving the Imams one receives *thawab*, great rewards in paradise. Besides the endless walls and ceilings of mirrors and immense crystal chandeliers, there are exquisite carpets throughout the enormous rooms. According to my hosts, the shrine of Imam Reza at Mashad completely sustains itself. There is a factory that makes the miles of carpets, and women donate gold jewelry to be melted down for the decorations of the tombs.

Before we went, our group was given a list of suggestions for our ziyarat. They are as follows:

1. [The pilgrim should] enter the holy shrine after performing wudu (ablution) or *ghusl* (bathing).

2. [The pilgrim should] wear clean, tidy, and new clothes.

3. While going toward the holy shrine, the pilgrim should walk with peace and dignity. The pilgrim should walk with humility by keeping the head down and should develop the concentration of mind and presence of heart.

4. In the holy shrine, the pilgrim should be busy praising the Creator, and the heart should remember the greatness of Allah. Pilgrim should continuously invoke blessings and salutations (salawat) upon the Holy Prophet of Islam (S.A.W.) and his Holy Ahl al-Bayt (A.S.).

5. In the holy shrine, the pilgrim should avoid vain talk and should abstain from altercation and hostile discussions.

6. The pilgrim, when reaching the precincts of the holy shrine, should stop and seek the permission of entry from the Holy Imams (A.S.).

7. The pilgrim should abstain from creating any sort of trouble in the holy shrine and should abide by the instructions of the attendants of the holy shrine.

8. When the pilgrim sees the holy burial chamber (*zarih*), before starting the recitation of ziyarah he should first recite Takbir i-e to recite Allah Akbar.

9. The Pilgrim should try his best to recite the ziyarah standing.

10. While reciting ziyarah the pilgrim's face should be directed towards zarih and for the supplication (du'a) the pilgrim should move toward the upper part of the zarih and recite the dua while facing the Qeblah.

11. The pilgrim should recite the ziyarah only narrated by the Holy Imams (A.S.) for example Ziyarat-i-Aminullah and Ziyarat-i-Jameh-i-kabeer, and should abstain from reciting any non-authentic and non-appropriate words in the ziyarah.

12. The pilgrim should not recite the ziyarah in a raised voice.

13. After the recitation of the ziyarah, the pilgrim should perform the two rakah Namaz-i Ziyarah and present the thawab (spiritual reward) of it to the Holy Imam (A.S.).

14. After the Namaz-i-Ziyarah the pilgrim should recite the recommended supplications (dua) and then should pray to Allah Almighty to grant everything

good and beneficial to his relatives, friends and all those who had requested him to pray for them in the holy shrine.

15. The pilgrim should recite the Holy Quran as much as possible and present the thawab of it to the holy soul of the Immaculate Imam (A.S.).

16. The pilgrim should pray to Allah Almighty to hasten the advent of Imam-i-Zaman Hadrat Mahdi (A.S.) and to grant prosperity and success to Islam and the Muslims in the world.

The shrine was glittering with gold and encrusted with jewels. Mrs. Mualana told me that women from all over the world had donated gold jewelry that was melted down and used to decorate the shrine. This lavish show of adoration of the Imams is sometimes criticized by other Muslims, and understandably so. They argue that gold should not be used to ritually adulate and commemorate Imam Reza, that he would have wanted the gold to be sold to feed the poor and care for the homeless. It reminded me of the arguments that some Christians have about the Vatican and the lavish lifestyles of its inhabitants. Wasn't the message of Jesus and of the Prophet Muhammad to help those in need and live modestly?

Imam Reza was the son of a very pious and dearly loved slave. His mother was married into the holy family and, as her mother-in-law predicted, would give birth to an Imam of great value. Shi'a believe that if one makes pilgrimage to Imam Reza's tomb, all sins will be washed away on Resurrection Day and the believer will be absolved and go directly to heaven.

Upon entering the women's section, I was amazed at how crowded it was. Still early in the day, there were thousands of women of all ages. They greeted me with smiles and, when they heard that I was an American, were especially kind. The female ushers, who looked like fairies dressed in black, waved neon green feather dusters to direct people to move. They would gently tap you on the shoulder to get you to keep moving, so as to prevent human traffic jams in the shrine. Their soft smiles and patience were amazing. Considering that they ushered women through the doors to the tomb, they were remarkably peaceful and elegant. People cuddled together with their children and friends, praying for what all humans of every religion pray for: to find a husband, have a child, heal an illness, receive the gift of prosperity, and ultimately for redemption and salvation. As we moved closer to the tomb, patience had run thin and women were desperately pushing. Bodies against bodies, we moved as one large unit trying to touch the tomb. It was a claustrophobic frenzy; we were pushed and shoved by women trying to stuff dollar bills through the openings. Trying to accrue thawab with these monetary donations, they had forgotten any good manners. Some women were muttering quiet prayers while others were sobbing loudly. My young roommate was overwhelmed with the crowd and what felt like hysteria. This was in sharp contrast to the rest of the building, which was profoundly peaceful.

One night I felt like everyone was staring at me. When we went back to the hotel I told my friends that I was surprised, because many people had mistaken me for an Iranian in the United States. They laughed and told me that people were staring at me because I was wearing makeup and it was wrong to be made up in the mosque. It was true: I had just showered and put on fresh makeup. I scrubbed it all off, but later that night we saw plenty of women wearing makeup and got a good laugh.

While we were in Mashad, our tour guide kept saying that we were going to be guests of Imam Reza for lunch. Although I knew that Imam Reza had been dead for centuries, I didn't initially realize that this was a metaphor. We went to the cafeteria that is attached to the shrine, with special tickets in our hands to eat blessed food. There were thousands of pilgrims patiently waiting in line. Some people approached us and started arguing with our guide, saying that it was unfair that people from all over the world could receive this holy food that brought good health and luck but because they were locals they couldn't get in. Our guide reminded them that as pilgrims we had traveled far, and for some of us this would be a once-in-a-lifetime opportunity. As we entered, I was amazed at how immaculately clean and organized everything was. All the servers were volunteers and the food was delicious. We ate and laughed and marveled at the degree of calm organization that prevailed as these volunteers fed ten to twelve thousand visitors each day.

As the days proceeded, most of the guys on our tour started to grow the classic Shi'a beard, an attractive five-day growth that was kept trimmed and neat. Some of us could easily pass as locals. While in Iran, I tried my best to blend in. One afternoon my friend and I went to an exquisite jewelry store. The shop specialized in recreations of antique Persian jewelry laden with rubies, emeralds, and sapphires. While we stood at the counter examining precious pieces, the man behind me looked at me in shock and asked if I was an American. When I answered yes, he asked what I was doing in Mashad. I said that I had come for pilgrimage. He smirked and emphatically stated, "Well, your government sure is fucked up!" I responded, "So is yours!" A huge smile spread across his face and he held up his hand to give me a high five. We all laughed and he asked me if I wanted to have some tea.

On one special evening, everything was open almost all night long. We had dinner at midnight. Schedules were created to support the prayer times and the pilgrims' needs. Everyone walked through the streets relaxed as if on holiday. Little girls wore pastel-colored satin chadors with lace and silk flowers sewn on the edges to frame their smiling faces. That night we walked to the tomb from our hotel, and I wore sandals. I forgot that I needed black socks because I was wearing nail polish. Before you enter the mosque you must remove your shoes, go through a security check, and leave cameras behind. We entered the women's entrance and the guard looked at my feet and wrinkled her nose, then shook her head and said something in Farsi, which my Pakistani friend translated. "You cannot enter with nail polish," she told me. "It is considered impure." Of course I knew that from many years ago, when I wore polish to the Shi'a school in California. How could I have forgotten? I said that I would go back to the hotel and get some socks.

My friend insisted that I take hers and she pulled them off, I slipped them on, and we went in to pray. We were not doing just the usual daily prayers but added many special prayers called du'as. As mentioned earlier, du'as are petitions of gratitude or requests of Allah. Often the Imams are asked to be intercessors for those in need or those seeking redemption. We would stand together with our fingers pointed toward the door to the shrine, and our guide, Mrs. Maulana, would read these special prayers from a book. The prayers were in Arabic, and often people looked at us as oddities, but they knew that we were there for the same reason that they were.

My favorite times in the shrine were when I was alone and I could sit and pray in my own way, marveling at the beauty of the world we live in. The diversity of spirituality, even within Islam, was astounding to me. Sitting alone, watching my breath and focusing on stillness and silence, I felt expanded and understood to some degree what *tawhid* means. For Muslims the concept of tawhid is the oneness of God, and in a sense, to me at least, it means that we are all connected, there is no separation between anything and God.

Soon our trip would come to an end. Honestly, I was tired of praying all day and night. Well, at least going through the motions. My prayers couldn't be uttered in Arabic, Farsi, or Urdu because I don't know any of those languages well. I was lucky to recite a few things in Arabic. But praying in Arabic has no meaning for me. Even prayers in English seem heady. My prayers are an outreach from my heart to the heart of God and are completely silent. They are a way to connect to the infinite source of life. For me, in Iran or at home, Islam has taught me to surrender, to trust, to have faith, and to bow down to the great mystery we call life. I am afforded to live in gratitude for whatever life brings.

As we got ready to leave Iran I had mixed feelings. I was ready to go home and see my family, but I wanted one last kebab. I was tired of Twelver Shi'ism, its rules and regulations, but loved the richness of the rituals. I was thankful to say that I am *mashtee*, an honorific title to those who make the pilgrimage to Imam Reza's tomb in Mashad. I was sad to say goodbye to people whose names I did not know and whom I would never see again. These people, who gave me free candy, fresh bread, and kisses on the cheek, would stay embedded in my heart forever. I would take with me the women at the shrines who hugged me, kissed me, wiped my tears, and tried to show me a way to God that they knew and cherished. These strangers took my hands, pushing through crowds, saying what, I am not sure; but many times a path in the crowd opened for me so that I could touch a shrine or kiss a relic. Their whispers of "Amreeki" showed me that these Shi'a women were nothing of what the average American views on television. I thank them for their patience.

As for my travel partners, I was sad to see our trip coming to an end. We had laughed and cried, rejoiced and complained together. In the end we agreed that a sense of humor prevailed as we used squat toilets and tripped on our long black chadors. On our last night in Iran we meandered through Mashad, eating last bites of bread and candy, purchasing one last scarf and some world-renowned saffron to take home as gifts. We all wanted to clean up before we got on the bus returning to the airport in Tehran. "Let's find a hammam" (a public bathhouse), someone suggested.

Looking for a hammam in that neighborhood proved disastrous. The one we found was the filthiest place I have ever seen. In absolute contrast to any other hammam I have visited, it was disgusting. Fortunately, there was hot water, so we showered and returned to the bus somewhat clean and refreshed. All the places we stayed in Iran were very clean and comparable to hotels found in the United States. I guess we made the wrong choice here. As we left the bathhouse grumbling and complaining, young boys with small boxes approached us. On each little box a bird was perched. When we paid the boys a few pennies, a tiny trained bird would reach down and pull out a card. Handwritten in Farsi, each card had a poem by the famous Persian poet Hafez. Considered good luck, we all purchased one and our gloom was transformed into love and gratitude.

This trip held tremendous personal meaning to me. It was the fulfillment of a dream that I had held for many years. As a teenager I wanted to go to Persia. Growing up in Alaska, I wondered what caused such a desire. It was when I entered the museum of Omar Khayyam that I had a sudden realization. There was the poetry that, as a young girl, I had loved so dearly. I had never really put the deeply religious Shi'a in the same container in which I had put Omar Khayyam, who wrote the *Rubaiyat*. Until I went to Iran I was unable to see how truly rich the country and the people are. Spending years at the Shi'a school in Los Angeles County had a tremendous effect on my worldview, as well as on my heart, but when I re-read the first stanzas of the *Rubaiyat* I remembered why I had such a fascination with Persian culture. Because I was traveling with extremely religious people, I missed a lot of Persian culture, such as the music and dance, which is often not seen during a religious pilgrimage. My companions were focused on a relationship with God through ritual and prayer rather than on the sensuousness of Persian culture, which has been oppressed by the highly religious government that runs Iran today. From my perspective, one can find God in all forms, whether in prayer or in music. It is the eyes and ears of one's heart that define the religious experience.

Of all the strong memories I have of my pilgrimage in Iran, the people are what stay in my heart more than the places. There was, however, one place that was my favorite. As we walked toward the site, there was a man sitting on the ground playing a *kamanche*, a four-stringed fiddle. It was the first time I had heard music in Iran, and the melody filled my heart with joy. The sun was bright, people were picnicking, and I was about to enter what would be my favorite place in Iran, the Harunieyeh tomb in Tus, where al-Ghazali is buried. At this site al-Ghazali met with his Sufi companions to pray and practice *dhikr*, beautiful chants and meditations to remember God. It is in this place, which was dry and dusty, a simple building with no mirrors, gold, or jewels, that Imam al-Ghazali, during his dark night of the soul, his doubt in God, experienced the light of God cast into his heart, making him a believer. Being a practicing Sufi myself, I was overcome with gratitude. In my own spiritual life it is this light that has kept me in relationship to the Divine. This profound infusion of grace, accompanied with stillness and love, has made me a believer. There are no threats of hell or rewards of heaven that make me who I am, but it is this experience of *uns*, the intimacy of God, that keeps my faith. As it says in the Qur'an, "God is as close to us as our jugular vein" (50:16).

When I realized that I was standing on ground where prayers were offered from the deepest part of the heart, I wept in reverence. I stood in a place where many people had pursued the love of God, and for me it was a delightful and humbling experience. Although my spiritual journey through Islam as I studied Sufism, its mystical side, is somewhat different from that of the Twelver Shi'a I worked and traveled with, I can only believe that, although our ways are different, our hearts end up in the same place. My years with the Shi'a community have left a seal on my heart. As I finish writing this book, I am left with a multitude of adventures and memories, new friends, and old acquaintances. I have watched young girls grow up and marry, older members of the community have died, and I have found a new community of Shi'a refugees in Nebraska, where I now live, with whom I am forming friendships. The next chapter of my life is a mystery that I bow down to with respect and faith. Every day brings new, unexpected turns. Tonight, I am invited to commemorate Arbaeen, the fortieth night after the death of Imam Husayn, with a group of Shi'a from Saudi Arabia who attend school at the University of Nebraska in Omaha. As I wrapped the long black scarf around my hair the phone rang. It was Mrs. Maulana. "Salaam, Sister Bridget. We are going to Iraq in December. Do you want to come?"

"Yes," I said, "Inshallah," God willing.

Glossary

Abaya – long overcoat

Adab – good manner, behavior

adhan – call to prayer

ahl al-bayt – the Prophet's immediate family (people of the house)

akhlaq – "Disposition, way of being

al-Abbas – the son of Imam Ali and Ummul Banin.

alams – standards with names and blessings of the martyrs

al- Ghazali – Sufi mystic and theologin

Ali Asghar – infant son of Imam Husayn

Aqiq – a garnet colored stone worn for good luck

Arbaeen – the fortieth day after Ashura

Asalaamu alaykum – may peace be upon you (greeting)

Ashura – the tenth day, commemorates the martyrdom of Imam Husayn

azadari – sorrow, practice of mourning

azadars – mourners

baraka – grace

chador – black tent like covering for women when outside of the home

dandia – Indian folk dance

deshdasha – long caftan typically worn by men

dhikr – the remembrance of God (chanted)

du'as – prayers other than obligatory ones

dupatta – scarf

Eid al-Adha – feast of the sacrifice following Hajj

Eid al-Fitr – feast at the end of the Ramadan fast

Fatima al-Zahra – daughter of the Prophet Muhammad

Fesenjoon – chicken cooked in pomegranate and ground walnut sauce

Five Pillars – are the framework of the Muslim life. They are the testimony of faith, prayer, giving zakat (support of the needy), fasting during the month of Ramadan, and the pilgrimage to Mecca once in a lifetime for those who are able.

Fulla – Muslim Barbie doll

hadith – written collection of the Prophet's sayings and behaviors

Hafez – Persian poet and mystic

Hagar – mother of the Ismaelites

hajj – the annual pilgrimage to Mecca

halal – permitted

hammam – bath house

haram – forbidden

Hassan – son of Imam Ali

Hazrat Abbas – son of Imam Ali (mother: Umul Bannin)

Hazrat Fatima – daughter of the Prophet Muhammad

Hijab – head covering

hip-hop – cultural American music movement

holy Imamate – Prophet Muhammad, Fatima and the twelve Imams

hookah – water pipe used for smoking scented tobacco

houza – religious school

Husayn – martyred son of Imam Ali, grandson of the Prophet Muhammad

hutba – sermon

ihram – the dress worn by male Muslims on their pilgrimage to Mecca, consisting of two white cotton cloths

Imam – for Shi'a, it is the term used for the descendants of the Prophet. For Sunni imams are community leaders and religious authorities

Imam Reza – eighth Imam

Imambargah – an altar or site where mourning rituals take place

Imams – the twelve infallible descendants of the Prophet

Isa – Jesus

Ithna Ashariya – Shi'a that follow the 12 imams

Jafaria – Pakistani Shi'a organization

jalous – procession

Jibril – Angel Gabriel

Jilbab – long dress

jinn – creatures named in the Qur'an made from a smokeless fire

Kaaba – the stone that Muslims circumnambulate during Hajj

kamanche – Iranian bowed string musical instrument

Karbala – The Battle of Karbala took place on Muharram 10, in the year 61 AH of the Islamic calendar (October 10, 680 AD) in Karbala, situated in present day Iraq.

Khadija – first wife of the Prophet Muhammad, mother of Fatima khums – one fifth of one's earnings given to charity

La ilaha illallah – there is no God but God

Mahram – male relative

Majlis – gathering

Maryam al-Kubra – Jesus' mother

mashtee – person who has made a pilgrimage to Mashad, Iran

masjid – mosque

matam – term used for the act of self-flagellation during the Shia Remembrance of Muharram

Muharram – first month of Muslim calendar alsoThe event that marks the anniversary of the Battle of Karbala when Imam Husayn

Mullah – religious leader

mut'a – temporary marriage

nazr – vow

nikkah – marriage- religious leader

niyyat – intention

noweh – cantor

Punjabi – reference to clothing style from India

Roqayyeh – daughter of Imam Husayn

Saddam Hussein fifth President of Iraq (1979 – 2003).

Sakineh – Imam Husayn's daughter

salawat – blessing of the Prophet and his family

sawm – a call for the blessing of the Prophet and his family

sayyed – descendant of the Prophet Muhammad

shafa'a – intercession

shahada – to bear witness

Shaytan – satan

Sofreh – table cloth, wedding food

sohan – Iranian candy made from honey, saffron

sunnah – the sayings and doingsof the Prophet

Ta'ziyeh – replicas of tombs

Tajweed- to improve, to make more beautiful

tasbeh – prayer beads

tawhid – the oneness of God

thawab – merit

turbah – small clay tablet made of soil from Karbala that Shi'a rest their foreheads on when praying

ulama – religious scholars

uns – intimacy

wudu – ritual washing before praying

Yazid – Caliph blamed for the death of Imam Husayn

Zakat – alms

Zakireh – women who recite the laments during a gathering

Zamzam – holy water

ziyarat – pilgrimage to holy sites

About the Author

Dr. Bridget Blomfield teaches Religious Studies and is the director of the Islamic Studies Program at the University of Nebraska-Omaha. She is also a faculty member of the International Studies and Women's Studies programs. Her areas of interest include women's religious rituals, and Islamic mysticism. As an ethnographer, she researches Shi'a and Sufi Muslim women and their religious commitments to Islam. Her personal life is dedicated to the pursuit of consciousness.

31901059345555